JUNIOR

JUNIOR
writing your way ahead in advertising
by Thomas Kemeny

with foreword by Jeff Goodby

pH **powerHouse Books** Brooklyn, NY

Junior: writing your way ahead in advertising

Text © 2019 Thomas Kemeny
Foreword © 2019 Jeff Goodby

Published in the United States by powerHouse Books,
a division of powerHouse Cultural Entertainment, Inc.
32 Adams Street, Brooklyn, NY 11201-1021

www.powerHouseBooks.com

Limit of Liability Disclaimer: Although the author has made every
effort to ensure that the information in this book was correct at press
time, the author and publisher do not assume and hereby disclaim
any liability to any party for any loss, damage, or disruption caused
by errors or omissions, whether such errors or omissions result from
negligence, accident, or any other cause.

Further, while every effort was made to make the information in here
useful, the author and publisher do not assume and hereby disclaim
any liability to any party for any financial or professional loss, damage,
or disruption caused by following the advice in this book. The book is
called *Junior* and thus all the information herein should be taken with
a grain of salt. Like seriously, the author is just one guy and he doesn't
even run an ad agency. Though he wants to be helpful, he's far from
perfect and following his advice blindly is probably not a good idea.
If you only read one book on advertising that you'll base all of your
decisions on, read another one. Don't bet your whole career or whole
business on what is said in here. Also, the author uses a few swear words.

To all lawyers and other people who love reading fine print, thank you
for taking the time to look at this. I hope you found it to your satisfaction.

First edition, 2019

Library of Congress Control Number: 2018961865

ISBN 978-1-57687-912-2

Book design by Anna Kasnyik - www.ksnyk.com

Printed by Asia Pacific Offset, Hong Kong

10 9 8 7 6 5 4 3

Printed and bound in China

To my loving wife, Jen:

yo!

Contents

People ask me all the time who my mentors were. I tell them they are people like Thomas Kemeny.

Thomas and his partner came into my office one day with an interesting idea for our "got milk?" campaign. "What if we made bus shelters that actually smelled like chocolate chip cookies," they gushed, "and then had a big 'got milk?' sign on the pack panel?"

I said it sounded great. How would we do it?

"We have no idea," they said.

I told them to come back with something we could actually do.

A week or two later, they walked in with the name of a company in New Jersey that made all-natural smells. Seriously. This place not only had a substance that smelled like chocolate chip cookies baking, they had several different chocolate chip cookie smells for us to sample, each based on a separate recipe.

Thomas was lit up. "We can put a big bar up in the back of the shelter that's infused with the smell! Try it," he said, handing me a little vial of the stuff. Indeed, it smelled great.

"As long as we don't get arrested," I said.

We did.

A few weeks later, I was told to go over to Union Square in San Francisco, where our flagship cookie smelling bus shelter had been installed. There were TV network trucks everywhere. It was a sensation.

The very next day, however, the city's board of supervisors shut all the shelters down, saying they'd received ongoing complaints from people who were allergic to cookies. One supervisor also said that the shelters were "cruel to underfed homeless people."

Thank you, San Francisco.

But actually this meant we got a whole new cycle of publicity. That night, Jay Leno said that the city's bus shelters could "now go back to smelling like urine."

The point is that advertising, at its best, is a little like vandalism. It's naughty, in your face, and still there the next day (unless the city takes it down). Shoot for that feeling. Look evilly forward to your creations being unleashed on the world. When you find people like me who champion such undertakings, use them mercilessly to achieve your ends.

One more thing before Thomas takes over here.

It's a business of rejection. You reject things in your own head. Then your partner rejects them. Then your client. And if you're lucky enough to get it all by them and out into the world, your friends and family and even people you haven't talked to in years go on to reject it.

Don't listen to them. Or if you have to listen to them because they are paying you, don't let them chip away at your idea. Start over. When you start over, in my experience, you almost always end up thinking how lucky you were to kill off that first idea. And in some instances, the threat of starting over for some reason causes the client to circle back to your first idea after all.

For instance, I told Thomas I might start over on this introduction, and he totally just bought it on the spot, right then and there.

You will learn a lot herein, unvarnished, and from the perspective of a thoughtful, reality-based, wise but not old mentor. As Yogi Berra might have said, I wish this book existed when I was you.

Get out there.

Jeff Goodby
San Francisco
August 22, 2018

This book represents my views and not those of my employers. Unless you like it, in which case they not only endorse it, but it was their idea.

In most agencies it's an insult. A slur. From the moment you get in, you want to kill that word off of your title. Murder it and have its body wash ashore in Baltimore. You try to mumble it in hopes that people will miss it. Scratch it off of forms so that others won't see it. Why won't it die? Make the hurt stop.

Junior.

It's also where the energy of an agency comes from. The title of the people willing to do anything it takes, anytime it takes. "Sure, I can work this weekend. I can just make it to my next kid's birth." Junior is the pulse. The youth and vibrancy. The bright-eyed, puppy-dog hope that refuses to be jaded by anything. The fight that makes the subhead on a banner as stellar as the TV spot. The heart.

In a perfect agency, we're all juniors.

This is your last chance to turn around.

Traditionally, advertising books have been written by people with established careers, big offices, and letters like "VP" in their titles. Superstars who've been working for several decades. They have stories from the old days when people could start in the mailroom. They're sagely CDs or ECDs. They are talented.

That's been done.

Who wants another book filled with seasoned wisdom? This is a book written by somebody still getting his bearings. Someone who has made an extraordinary number of errors in a still short career. Someone who has managed to work at some of the best agencies in the world despite these shortcomings.

Hi. I'm Thomas.

This book is not a retrospective from some ad legend. This is not a book for clients or our bosses. It's a book that should be instantly useful for people starting out. A guide for the first few years at a place you'd actually want to work.

Advertising books haven't been written by people who deal with banners, social media post copy, print ads in local papers, etc. I did. You will.

This is a book for the years in the trenches. The all-nighters. The years where you are making something out of nothing seven days a week, because you're lucky to even be given nothing.

By way of disclaimer I'll mention that my way into advertising was a strange one. It didn't involve friends in the business, portfolio schools, nepotism, or secret society membership. I didn't kill or sleep with anyone (not for my career anyways). I got in because I worked like a mule and did what I'll talk about in the following pages.

Some of the things I did were smart. A lot of the things I did were stupid. Clearly I did enough things right, but in all honesty I made and continue to make more than my share of mistakes. And some of my biggest mistakes have led to my greatest successes. Learn from mine and perhaps you can find bigger and better mistakes to make.

This book is my personal perspective (shaped of course by those around me), but I don't blame anyone else for my views. Nor should you.

Alright then, enough dicking around. Welcome to advertising. Grab some leftover pizza from the kitchen and let's get to work.

A needlessly specific story
about how to get in.

In case you're one of those
go-getters who got this book
before you got a job.

(hint: lead with your balls).

At Crispin Porter+Bogusky in 2005, they had a full-wall bookcase filled with prospective employee portfolios. Hundreds. One day I asked the recruiter, "Are those all the portfolios you guys have been sent this year?" She told me, "No. Those are just the portfolios worth hanging onto."

Do something big, or you'll just be another "maybe" in that wall of portfolios. Need an example of how to get in? Keep reading.

(Internship phone call)

"Hi Veronica, this is Thomas Kemeny."

"…"

"I emailed you and you said to send my book.
Have you had a chance to look at it?"

"It's here somewhere."

"Oh…"

"…"

"…"

"Tell you what, why don't you send me a letter about
why you want to intern at Crispin Porter + Bogusky."

"Ok."

Dear Veronica,

Why I want to work at Crispin Porter + Bogusky

I'm sick of people asking to see my ads. Friends, family, co-workers, instructors, everyone is always curious what new ideas I've come up with. I've had strangers come up to me and tell me they've heard about an ad I did, and that they want to see it. It's becoming a nuisance, and I think CP+B is the solution.

If I intern there then I can say to people, "Go pick up *Rolling Stone*, and you'll see the ad I made." Or "See that ad in *Rolling Stone*? I got a low-fat organic cranberry scone for the guy who came up with that."

So why would I choose CP+B over another agency? Because you produce ads that aren't culturally null. And your agency creates ads that are appreciated by non-advertising people, and that's what I try to do.

Why you should want to hire me

I could say that I'm smart, dedicated, reliable, honest, ridiculously nice, pleasant, easy to be around, etc., because it's all true. However, I think I'll focus on the really important issue—I don't smell bad.

I'm sure you've gotten lots of letters from lots of people who want to intern there, and I'm positive that none of them have mentioned how they smell. Now, I'm not implying that they do smell, but keep in mind that you're running the risk. So I'm going to let you know right off the bat that I don't.

Why not to hire me

Why should you have to waste your time thinking of reasons not to hire me? I figured I'd save you some time, and give you a list.

I have really bad handwriting (I know you can't tell here, but it's really bad.)
I live in Chicago (and what kind of lunatic would be willing to go to Florida in the heart of summer for an unpaid internship?)
I don't go to a portfolio school (so how can I be expected to create ads that look like everyone else's?)

In closing

I hope you hire me, and not just somebody from a portfolio school. Heaven help advertising if even CP+B becomes predictable.

I love you guys,
Thomas Kemeny

Hi Thomas,

I liked your letter. Do we already have your mini-book here? If not then please send it over—I'd love to see your work. Are you a writer?

Thanks!

Veronica

Dear Veronica,

I'm glad you liked my letter. To answer your questions,
1.) Yes you do have my book but it's not mini, it's a gaudy 8.5 × 11 thing, because
2.) Yes, I am a writer, and the copy would be hard to read if it were small. It looks like a standard, blue school notebook with writing on it. I hope you like my work, and I apologize for the extra space it may be taking up on your desk. Contact me if you need me to send another one, or for any other reason.

-Thomas Kemeny

OOOOOH, that book. I do have it. It's on my desk. Cool. I'll get back with you in about a week.

Thanks!

:)

Veronica

...

Dear Veronica,

This is the student from Chicago who doesn't smell bad and doesn't go to a portfolio school. I wrote a letter a while back about why I want to work there and why you should hire me. I also happened to write why you shouldn't hire me. Being an unfortunately persuasive writer, I must've convinced you too well that I shouldn't work there, because I am still in Chicago.

I must admit that this was not in fact my intention. I actually wanted to work there. I thought this message was conveyed properly when I received an enthused e-mail from you asking to see my work. Then everything got hazy.

I can't help feeling like a stranded puppy (search Getty Images for "sad puppy" if you need reference). I never got an official rejection, or advice, or an internship, or a rabid koala. I wasn't expecting the koala, but I would have liked to receive one of the others. It might be in part because I never gave a land address, but I never got an e-mail or phone call either.

I still think I'd be a good writer because I write ads that are inside of the box (everyone seems to be moving outside of the box so the rent is pretty cheap and it's roomier). I also found that I have other qualities that I didn't mention in the last letter.

Reasons to still hire me:
1. I'm persistent
2. I'm tall (so I can take down cookie jars that may be lingering just out of reach, and let's face it, what good is a creative department without cookies?)
3. I'm easy to get along with. Way easier than a Russian dictator (who I don't recommend you guys hire even if you don't hire me. You hire him and next thing you know you'll all be wearing those funny fur hats, and then the PETA people will be all over you.)
4. I'm not a professional boxer. (Other people applying might be, and while it might seem like a good idea, it could cause problems. Just try telling Evander Holyfield that his copy needs work.)

To be fair I also found more reasons why you still shouldn't hire me.

Reasons you still shouldn't hire me:
1. I keep giving you reasons not to hire me.
2. My handwriting is getting worse and worse (I mentioned this in the last letter, but these scrawls are getting pretty ridiculous. I had to buy the Rosetta stone just so I could find out what I myself was writing.)
3. I sent you my book two months ago, and now that book is 2 months old. And what kind of person sends a book that's 2 months old?

I'm still interested in CP+B and I would like to give you a revised copy of my book.

Let me know if you're curious. If not, here's where you can send the rejection letter:

555 Smith St.
Chicago, IL 60613.

Thank you,

-Thomas

Dear Veronica Padilla,

I still haven't heard back from you, so I'll assume that you've all been kidnapped by pandas. I'll also assume that they stole your computers and that you would probably want me to reattach the letters I've written you in case you escape. You'll probably want at least one work sample as well, so I've attached that too. Thanks

-Thomas

Thanks for your concern. The Pandas decided to set me free. I'll be in touch soon. I need some time to recoup.

:)

Veronica

Dear Veronica,

This is the guy from Chicago that doesn't smell bad, doesn't go to portfolio school, and is not a professional boxer. We have e-mailed back and forth several times now, and it has recently come to my attention that I still don't work at CP+B. I've been trying to figure it out for a while and I think I've finally isolated the problems:

1. I write too much (I mean, this is advertising, what business does a copywriter have writing so many words? And in Times New Roman!! Has nobody told me that's not allowed?)
2. I have not proven my pie-eating ability (and when those jerks from that law firm burst into the agency with a hundred pies and challenge the creatives to a pie eating contest to the death, how do you know I can hold my own?)
3. You've never seen me, so how do you know I'm not ugly or that I don't have a robotic arm?

4. You don't know if I can handle the serious workload of your agency (working late, waking up early, pulling all-nighters, writing all the time, sometimes not having time to eat.)
5. I've never told you anything I do outside of advertising (so how do you know I can keep up an interesting conversation while the rest of the hostages sneak out the door?)

Well, let me resolve these issues for you:

1. I don't have to write so much. I can stop in the middle of
2. Sure I'm skinny, but I can pack away a fair number of pies.
3. How dare you call me ugly and draw attention to my robotic arm?
4. I'm finishing a 4-year college. I know all about not sleeping, working hard, missing meals because I'm on a roll writing, losing all my work at 5 a.m. that's due at 8 a.m. This is nothing new to me. I look forward to the craziness.
5. I have lots of things I do other than advertising. I cook awesome food and love learning facts about different dishes and ingredients, I play guitar, I write short stories, I run and cycle, I draw (mostly in charcoal), and I smile and spread my cheer. Actually, one of the reasons I'm in advertising is because I'm interested in everything else in the world too.

I'd love to work at CP+B, and I know I'd get along really well with everyone. Maybe I could be flown down there sometime (if I can sneak my robotic arm through customs that is).
Regardless, get in contact with me. We'll talk advertising, reminisce on our past communications and plot our revenge against the pandas,

-Thomas

Dear Veronica,

So this is letter number I don't know, and I still haven't gotten a final yes or no. I think it might have something to do with the font I'm using. You see, CP+B has gotten so used to people kissing their ass and treating them like royalty, that they only respond to *this font* anymore. I don't mean it as a criticism; the praise is certainly well deserved. You guys are unbelievably good (thus my steady stream of emails). I think your agency can successfully keep from getting weighed down by your egos. Remember, that's how the Titanic sank.

Still, the last CP+B campaign I saw was the ----- ads, and they don't meet up with your usual quality of work. I mean, the execution was decent, but the strategy? come on! What was it: "Men need to act like sexist wolverines"? Is that original at all? It's the same strategy as that PSA for "The Preservation of Sexist Wolverines Coalition."

Part of this is me being bitter that some of my work doesn't meet up to most of your agency's work, and part of it is me being hurt that I still haven't gotten a response from you. I'm sure you've been really busy, and that hundreds of arrogant copywriters send you e-mails every day, but I was enjoying being sort of pen pals, because above being a good writer, I'm also a nice guy.
So to get back to where we should be:

Last we talked you were being kidnapped by pandas, I was busy not smelling bad, and we were sharing laughs about creative departments needing tall people to get cookies (remember those sweet memories? Beautiful times).

I've given you enough reasons to hire me, and even more reasons not to hire me, (like that crappy portfolio I sent you, and almost insulting CP+B at the beginning of this letter).

Sure, I've got lots to learn, but I'm a quick learner (minus my unwillingness to learn that I write too much, and that I shouldn't insult the people I admire and respect so much). I'd be thrilled if you took a look at my new book, even if just to find comfort in the fact that I'm just some arrogant non-portfolio school kid who doesn't even print on glossy paper. Don't be afraid to tell me no, I'll try writing you again in about a year when my book is even better.

In case all you could read of this letter was the words "this font" then trust me that the rest was awesome.

-Thomas Kemeny

Hi Thomas,

I'm a sucker for relentless persistence and am impressed by the giant cajones you must have to write such a letter.

I do believe you to be smarter than the average bear. This in fact, was just your way of getting attention. Probably hoping that I would forward this along to the Creative geniuses behind the ----- work. So that you could then create a dialogue with someone other than me.

I really like your letters. I can't offer you a job. I can offer you an internship. Let me know if you have any interest and I'll fill you in on the details. Please resend your mini book too, I'd like to revisit it.

:)
V

How to "hypothetically" live at the office for two weeks without anyone noticing:

Step 1
Intern at a place where it's not weird to see people at 4 a.m.

Step 2
Make a bed out of leftover foam from a giant hamburger costume.

Step 3
Put a giant chicken poster over your office window.

Step 4
Become friends with the security guard.
His name is Henry.

Step 5
Work until everyone leaves.

Step 6
Start working again before anyone gets in.

Step 7
Shower at the office gym.

Step 8
Eat free breakfast in the kitchen.
I recommend the croissants.
You know, hypothetically.

HOW I WENT FROM IDIOT INTERN
TO IDIOT PROFESSIONAL

To: Bob_Winter, John_Matazak

Hey!

So I met this guy Kevin, and told him I was hoping to move out to the West Coast to work. He gave your names as good people to contact. I was a former intern at Crispin Porter + Bogusky before freelancing around Chicago for about 2 months. Goodby Silverstein & Partners is high on my list of awesomeness (right under pre-foamed soap) and I'd love it if somebody out there could take a look at my book and give happy words to the recruiter/hr person that will make them give me a phone call where they yell a bunch of numbers at me. But baby steps... first let me say hi and send you my resume. Thanks,

-Thomas

The original message was received at Fri, 9 Dec 2005 11:44:59 -0800 from zproxy.gmail.com [64.233.162.199]

  ----- The following addresses had permanent fatal errors -----
<John_matazak@gspsf.com>
  (reason: 550 John_matazak@gspsf.com unknown user account)

  ----- Transcript of session follows -----
... while talking to [10.0.0.94]:
>>> DATA
<<< 550 John_matazak@gspsf.com unknown user account
550 5.1.1 <John_matazak@gspsf.com>... User unknown
<<< 554 no valid RCPT address specified

Final-Recipient: RFC822; John_matazak@gspsf.com
Action: failed
Status: 5.1.1
Remote-MTA: DNS; [10.0.0.94]
Diagnostic-Code: SMTP; 550 John_matazak@gspsf.com unknown user account
Last-Attempt-Date: Fri, 9 Dec 2005 11:45:06 -0800

From: Bob_Winter:

Thomas,

sure – you bet. send it on.

i`ll throw the happy words at you and matejczyk will throw the numbers.

some words i`m thinking about:

speculum.
nutsack.
vienna sausage.
shorn.
brazillian.
edward.

talk soon
b
————

To: Bob_Winter

Thanks Bob!

Excellent. I like edward and speculum the best so far, but I was thinking groupings of words (ie: thigh bone, anvil dent, Prince of Wales, etc.) here`s my book.

Also, a guy I worked with at Crispin Porter + Bogusky told me to contact Mike there as well. Do you mind forwarding this on to him as well? I don`t know if you have some fierce rivalry, and judging by my luck e-mailing Matejczyk, he`s probably got a silent Q or X or something.

Thanks,

–Thomas "What`s with this kid, like is he stupid?" Kemeny

To: John_Matejczyk, Bob_Winter

This is the mandatory "1 week follow-up" e-mail they told us we have to do in all my classes (ah, the wonderful insights, I almost don't mind paying for it for the rest of my life).

I'm sure you've just been busy either a) doing awesomeness for "the man" or b) stacking water cups to make a giant mural that says "hire Thomas" with dragons shooting flames on either side. I hope for b.

Let me know what you're thinking.

-Thomas

From: John_Matejczyk,

Hey Tom.

give me the mandatory post holidays follow up. buried now.

thanks.

-John

From: Bob_Winter

hey man - sorry for the lag time here. trying to think of new ways to say suck-y. how about El Sucko.
No, i liked your work quite a bit. in fact, send me a physical copy and i'll give it on to linda harless. she is the creative recruiter. don't hold your breath because i haven't heard of them looking for people, but if they like it something could happen down the line. we might win a cool new piece of business, or who knows maybe i'll completely tank and they'll fire me and then my salary will free up.

i also sent it to matejjjykkkkkch. and mike.

talk soon.
b

To: Bob_Winter

No problem. I'll print up a copy and tell Pablo to get the horses ready for the Pony Express.

Thanks for everything, and hopefully we'll be in touch,

-Thomas

To: Linda_Harless

Hey Linda,

Just following up to see if you've had a chance to set up the interview dates. I'm the ex-CPB intern guy with the square portfolio that had Bob Winter pass you my book.

Best,

-Thomas

From: Linda_Harless

I'm pleased to say we can use you as fast as I can get you out here.

Maybe Tuesday?

Writing.
Rewriting.
Re-rewriting.

Say hello to 90% of your job.

Hats off to ad schools because they have done a great job of teaching big ideas. It's rare to meet a creative who can't come up with a clever insight.

But, the majority of our job is not coming up with ideas. It's crafting the words and art around your and other people's ideas.

Ideas will move your career forward, but no matter how gigantic your ideas, you will have to write. I can't state enough how much you will be writing. To use myself as an example, in my first year I filled a notebook every other week (and I mostly use the computer). At some point your hand will hurt from writing.

Make peace with this fact and writing doesn't have to be the "other part" of your job. Writing can be ideas too. A great headline is always the byproduct of smart thinking. The next few pages are what I've learned about this freeing type of writing. How to make it shorter and better. How to make it longer and more interesting. How to have a f"*&ing g@@d time w/ punctuation! How to move people and make them feel stuff in their stomachs and heads. And how to make body copy that doesn't suck. And legal copy that's enjoyable. And a ton of other tricks. In other words, how to not be a shitty writer and enjoy your job.

Knowing how to get a brilliant line after a week is different than being a full-fledged copywriter. You will be doing ten times as much work at an agency as you did in school. Then you will redo that work to incorporate comments from the creative director, your client, the account team, strategists, research, and legal. And then your creative director again. "This reads like a lawyer wrote it." You will have times when you do a line in an hour. Or right then with the creative director looking at you.

Moral of the story: there's no waiting for inspiration.

The faster you can craft, the more time you'll have for blue-sky thinking. Because they sure as hell aren't putting time into the schedule for that. You got that space-cowboy? We've got deadlines to meet.

Early on in my career I was working on a new client pitch. I came in at 8:30 a.m. one morning and Rich Silverstein was already in the office, but nobody else.

"Hey, what do you do?"
"I'm a copywriter."
"Great." he said as he handed me a sketch. "Do a line for that."

A half hour later he called me into his office. He put the headline I gave him onto the ad.

"Eh, it's too long. Think of a shorter one."

He then politely tapped the lid of his marker on the table as he waited for me to write a new line on the spot.

REPEAT:
"I WILL NOT WRITE HEADLINES."

You know those sleazy lines that sound like they should be followed by a frat boy yelling "ZING!"? Don't write them. If you can hear a used car dealer saying it, unless that's your concept, don't write it. Make it juicy and fun, but not "you just got headlined!"

It's tough not to write something obvious, but here's a simple trick: Write until you go stupid. Sit in front of a page and write and write and write, line after line in quick succession until your lines are loosely connected to where you started. If you're writing about shoes, your headline topics may go like this: shoes, shoes, shoes, feet, feet, walking, walking, running, running and walking, long walks, thousand mile journeys, centipedes, animals wearing shoes, vanilla ice cream. Write until you hit vanilla ice cream, because soon after your subconscious will throw a gem at you, and buried in a list of lines that are weird and occasionally don't even make sense, you will find a line so deep and perfect that you'll wonder where it came from. You'll cover up the page, hoping that nobody realizes that you stole the line from your subconscious and you didn't actually have anything to do with it. Shhh, don't tell anyone. Nobody will know but us. I've been stealing lines from my subconscious my whole career. I haven't written a damn thing myself.

You'll know when you have a great headline because your pupils will dilate, you'll burst into laughter, your palms will sweat. You will look at the line and think "There is no better headline in the universe!!"

Then, once it can't possibly be any better, you want to take that one perfect line and rewrite it 20 different ways. Flop the structure. Start with the verb. Start with the noun. Play. Play. Play.

It's a lot of work, but it's fun if you do it this way. Plus, you're not doing the work anyway, you're just letting your mind float and stealing words it comes across. Isn't theft fun?

Headline:
As a company we're proud to support diversity and individuality.

Headline??:
Never hide your true identity unless you can fly or bend steel.

From their very origin, words were created to express ideas. Why is it then that we ever see ads with words just thrown together? Our own kind has created paragraphs that contain zero meaning. We have murdered those words. Those words' poor families will never feel their warm breath against their skin again. Why have you forsaken them? Please make sure your words have purpose. Think before you write. Nothing, said well, is still nothing.

A series of words:
Watch golf all day every day with On Demand golf.

An idea:
St. Andrews, always open for worship.

WRITE LIKE YOU WRITE.

The classic rule is to write like you talk. Unfortunately this cuts out letting you play with spelling, punctuation, capitalization, double meanings, abbreviations, layout, structuring, etc. I'm going out on a limb here and assuming that you write Facebook statuses, tweets, emails, texts, instant messages, captions, and scribble little notes. If you're like most young people you probably write more in a given day than talk. That's how we communicate these days. That's how people read. That's how you can write. Why write like you talk? Who talks anymore?

Line you could say:
It's what CEOs read.

Line that only works if you see it:
Thanks.
                    –The management

THESE WORDS HAVE BEEN KILLED BY ADVERTISING.

Use them sparingly
or ironically:

PERFECT
UNIQUE
INTERESTING
NEW
NO WONDER
SPECIAL
NOT TO MENTION
THAT'S WHY
FIRST
ONLY
EXCLUSIVE
SPECIAL
NO MATTER

A HEADLINE LIVES BEYOND
ITS WORD COUNT.

If you've painted the whole picture in five words, it's a pretty boring picture. Headlines are stories. Or rather, headlines tease at stories. Some aspect of them lingers in your mind.

A proper line leaves you dumbfounded. It slaps you. Punches you in the gut. You can't help but keep thinking about it. You want to tell others. You want to re-read it. You want to see what's in the body copy (surely the answer must be there).

The problem many copywriters make is that they write headlines that are eerily contained. They finish the second you reach the period.

But ads want to be memorable so the thought makes it to the product shelf. The words need to leave your mind drifting. They introduce a bigger world or a silly thought.

And here comes the contradiction: sometimes a headline can stay quiet. If you've got a complicated visual or idea, find the simplest, cleanest way to say what you have to, and get out.

Boring:
Fast has a new name.

Interesting:
Fast has a new name and it's Walter. We're very Walter.

Is the voice of the ad Winston Churchill? Homer? Snoop Dogg? Socrates? A cool uncle? Grandpa?

Give your words a perspective. Think about where it's coming from and where it's going. Everyone talks about knowing your target, but you also want to know your voice as the author. Otherwise your ads start sounding like they're coming from the Great Ad-Voice in the Sky down to the anonymous masses.

Before you ever put pen to paper, think about how you're going to say what you're saying. Sometimes when I want to write poetically I'll do a little theatrical flair with my hand in the air as I grab for the words. It puts my head where I want it to be.

If you were going for a worldly gentleman tone instead of saying "A is like B" you might say "A is not unlike B."

With that said, I've found that when I simply let go and just write as myself, honestly, purely, that all the CDs and clients say "Oh, this is totally in the voice of the brand." Go figure.

No voice:
The new no-glare tablet. Take work out of the office and into the sun.

With voice:
The new tablet. Embrace the light my office brethren.

DON'T LIE OR EXAGGERATE,
JUST REFRAME UNTIL YOU WIN.

The FCC lets you get away with a lot of lies. The public will not. People can see right through an exaggerated claim, and while it might make them react, it won't make them believe. Honesty is powerful stuff though. Of course, what truth you show is up to you. It's your ad. That means it's your game to create; feel free to nudge the rules until they're in your favor.

If you say your product is better and it's not, you'll be found out. If you say your product does something it doesn't do, you'll be sued. If your product is the best on the third Wednesday of every month, don't convince people it's always the best, you just have to convince people that the only day that matters is the third Wednesday of every month.

A poignant, honest line will feel bigger and live longer.

Nobody likes a liar. Your ad may be smart, even funny, but it will never make you feel warm if you're lying. You will do a lot of disgusting things in this business, but nobody can make you write a lie.

Issue to work around:
Your client makes a luxury car, but they don't fit in the luxury category.

Reframing until you win:
No matter how much they pad
the seats, some of us will never be
comfortable in a Lexus.

The telltale sign of a student ad is that it focuses on the problem. For example, a print ad for Thompson's Water Seal might show Lincoln's log cabin leveled to the ground with the line "Wetness can ruin."

The ad may be cute, but the takeaway is a fact I already know and tells me nothing about why I should buy the product. "Oh I get it, the product does the opposite of what I'm seeing??" Uninterestingly, I also know that Water Seal seals out water.

It's in the name. You've wasted an entire page to tell me that the product doesn't do what you showed me, but does do what the product name is. Great. Thanks.

Focus on the problem:
Made without gross artificial ingredients with names you can't pronounce.

———————————————————

Focus on the solution:
Start with the finest ingredients. Stop.

Ads are a terrible place to look for inspiration. For starters, they're already ads. They're also dull and have been flattened at least one round by a client. And most of them, even award winning ones, are not very impressive.

Literature is a great place to look for reference. It is rich with intriguing language. Trees don't blow in the wind, they wave their branches. Winter isn't cold, it climbs into your bones and settles its icy body. Use their tricks, dig up their secrets.

A line:
The most advanced electronic braking technology like Traction Control, ABS, and brake-force distribution.

———————————————————

A story:
The machines have taken over and they're fiddling with your brakes.

Metaphors, for example, are a great way to make your headlines interesting. All the greats do it. If you're talking about soft skin, you're boring. If you're talking about the delicate face of a far-off princess, you're interesting. Make your headline grand. Make it about a bigger truth. If your headline only exists within the ad, your ad will feel small.

Remember, a headline is a story. It goes somewhere.

LIKE, STUFF, AND THINGS.

Take these three words out of your headlines and your headlines will be better. Real authors rarely use them.

LIKE

I'm sure your teachers yelled at you in high school for using this word where it didn't, like, belong, but that's not my issue with it. Similes are just not as cool as metaphors. They're "like" the thorn in the rose of your headline. They make me want to rip my eyeballs out "like" grapes and mash them into wine. Lines without "like" are more interesting.

Take the following line: "The X3000 sports car is powerful like a lion." This line reads smarter as: "The lion under the hood of the X3000 sports car." Find ways to write out "like" and you'll be happier with the result.

STUFF

This is a great word to use in copy if you want to come across as flaky. If your plan is to sound like a dipshit then "stuff" is the word you want.

What are the things? If there is no answer then the word doesn't belong there. If the "things" are something specific then why don't you use the word of what the things are?

Move a step further or a step closer. Overstate, understate. Find the balance, skew the balance. Push your headlines in all sorts of different dimensions.

If you're selling whitening toothpaste, you don't have to say, "your teeth will be bright like light bulbs," you can say, "James, your smile is needed at the lighthouse." Sometimes you'll have moved too far away and your line will mean nothing—"James is in the lighthouse. Buy toothpaste"—and you'll need to move closer again.

Sometimes a line written one way is terrible, but you move a word, kill a word, switch a word, and it's brilliant. If it feels like there's an idea there, keep noodling. Maybe you'll find it.

Line:
A color printer for the price of black and white.

Stepping further
Millions of colors for the price of two.

You've got to write body copy. Body copy is often where people hide their natural headlines. They bury them somewhere between line 8 and 12. Try and write a lot of long copy and you might just recognize a line that will become the new headline.

And don't erase. Keep them there, even if only to remind yourself that one direction doesn't work. Maybe you'll look back on it later and it'll make you think of a new thought. Maybe it won't, but at least you can point to it and tell your partner or CD:

"I've totally been working, I mean, look at all these words."

First line:
Pause live TV. Never miss a game winning basketball moment.

Line found in copy:
And with one second left, he goes to the kitchen.

I was meeting with a well-respected copywriter many years ago when I was a student and he paused in the middle of reviewing my book. A look formed on his face not unlike the kind you'd make after being wrapped in a warm blanket, and he said:

"You know what? I like puns."

Puns are basic. Easy. Cheesy. And frankly they can be lame. But sometimes that's just what is called for. Not even intelligent puns. Bad puns. Painfully bad. So bad they're funny again. Played right they can remind you of childhood jokes you read on Popsicle sticks. And by being young and playful they can work magic by making a giant evil mega-corporation seem like a big toddler that you just can't stay mad at. Not an easy trick.

However, I've also found that behind most pun-lines, there are real headlines trying to get out.

When you find yourself looking at a pun that just seems too perfect to be true, scratch it out and keep writing. More often than not, the reason the pun works is because there's a truer and deeper thought to your concept. There will be a brilliant line that accomplishes the same effect that you thought only the pun could. And when you find it, it'll feel amazing. And you'll realize how much smarter your ad feels. How much smarter you feel.

Plus, the entire industry is pun-phobic and you can now safely show that piece to a creative director who read somewhere that puns are bad and thus won't even look at an ad that has a pun in it.

Line:
With this much power, you'll love it more than your family.

Yes, a pun:
"Sweetie, I can't get you a pony because I got 360 for myself."

Some writing is so liquid smooth that any attention paid to it slips right off. I've heard them called "Teflon ads" or "creative wallpaper."

Break the language. If you're writing a line a certain way because you think it's the right way to say something, it's the wrong way to say something.

When you've been studying advertising for a long time it becomes easy to know what the "right" word is. You know exactly what needs to be there for the client to be happy and for the meeting to be short. It's better to take the extra time and struggle to throw in a bogey. It rattles around in people's skulls and gets stuck.

Just do it.   ⟶   Just do sports.

Let's Motor.   ⟶   Let's Drive.

Got Milk?   ⟶   Do You Have Milk?

BATTLES RAGE WITHIN
THE HEADLINE.

To create tension in an ad you must create opposing forces. Sometimes the tension exists within the ad, contrasting good and bad, two ideas forced together that don't belong or are naturally contentious (hot and cold, angels and devils, engineers and rock stars). Sometimes the tension exists between the ad and the viewer, a sensitive topic, a challenge to the viewer or controversy. Sometimes the tension is created between the viewers, two opposing sides that people choose from that will make them enemies. Tension is intriguing; it gives people a thought to react to. It also gives them an excuse to care.

Dull line:
Take your work out of the office with a mobile broadband card.

Line with tension:
The office is no place to work.

THROW A WRENCH
AT YOUR BRAIN.

If you're having trouble it's easy to think it's because the assignment is too hard. Maybe it's because it's too easy. Try messing with yourself. Forbid the use of some letter of the alphabet. Or try not to use the word "the." As much as we love and desire freedom, we also need structure and rules to be productive. Ideally, you're the one making the boundaries and rules. That way you'll bitch about them less.

Restriction free boring line:
We want to show the world that America still makes great cars.

Writing a patriotic car headline without mentioning America or car:
Proof our flag was still there.

Editing isn't just about taking out the unnecessary words; sometimes it's about taking out words that are part of the meaning and seeing if the line evolves. Take a boring line and chop at it. See what words you can yank out.

Also, see if you can yank out punctuation. Smash two lines into one line. I hate it when I see lines with this structure: "Product line. Joke line." I could write 1,000 of these in an hour for any product and not one would be stellar. Seriously.

Here's five I came up with in 30 seconds. Time me:

It's the fastest processor out there.
Cheetahs buckle up.

The fastest processor on Earth.
Jupiter, you're next.

Lightning fast processing.
Thunder not included.

Blazing speeds for processing.
Check your smoke detector.

Fast processing. No brakes.

Condensing, shortening, and editing isn't about making the copy less to read, it's about making any length of copy more interesting to read. If you've written 100 headlines, try rewriting them by crossing out words.

HOW TO CHEAT LIKE A PRO.

Writing a brilliant headline takes time and thought. A luxury you will not have at 3 a.m. with the CCO awaiting your email. What can you do?

Fortunately there are some sneaky little copywriter tricks. They're not as effective as real, thought-out lines, but they work in a pinch.

1. You find a well-known saying and twist it.

Here are two examples of how you might tweak classic sayings to be about a wrinkle cream:
"Start acting your younger age."
"Make your long story look short."

2. Be bland, then play with it.

This: Great signal in Kansas City.
becomes: KC's drenched in our sweet and tangy signal sauce.

3. Take the crappy line from the creative brief and make it not shitty.

Some planners think long and hard about a strategic line. There will already be a great idea there that they are PRAYING you will use. Re-write it to be palatable and not only will it coast through internal meetings, but people will think you're super smart for listening to them.

4. Big/Small, High/Low

Clients love this shit. It's cheap, but it works. Find some parallel you can make in the language between opposites. You can do this with just about any brief, any client, any offer. For example, a bank wants you to talk about their low interest rates on their platinum cards. Your line can be "Small rates. Big deal." Or "Pay a little, get a lot." If you're working on a car you could say "Roars like a lion, priced like a lamb." Or "Giant horsepower. Tiny price." These lines almost always sell.

5. Duck. Duck. Goose.

You have two thoughts quickly and one longer thought.

"It's adjective. It's
It's going to change
something product

There's also a variation on it that's

"word, word, word,

Once you know this you will start seeing these lines everywhere. They're super simple and lots of agencies live by them.

other adjective.
the way you something
forever."

twist."

I'm not a fan of taglines. Firstly, I like taking out elements that aren't necessary and taglines are rarely necessary. Secondly, a lot of taglines exist to explain the joke because the headline and the visual aren't cutting it. They're clean-up lines. They're there because the rest of the communication has failed.

A tagline should be able to anchor an entire company. You should be able to put it on business cards, new employee handbooks, on delivery trucks, and then finally, yes, on ads. Look at any taglines you write. Would you hang your empire on it?

In high school we all learned the proper forms, structures, phrasings, etc., for "good writing." We learned how to set up a thesis, support it with three main points, and then summarize it in the conclusion. This is useful to know, but it is no longer the best way to communicate. Just as art styles change and evolve, so do writing styles. We've evolved beyond the basic structures a while ago. People absorb information differently. There are non-linear ways to present thoughts now. Tangents have become not only acceptable, but expected. "And" can start a sentence. Flow and style mean as much as being proper and organized. People want to be entertained when they read. The Language Police have been disbanded.

It's kind of an exciting time to be a writer. English is going through a major change. It's becoming flexible (even more than it always was). The writers have gotten fed up with the status quo of writing. Which is pretty sweet.

You're the new generation defining this language. Play around with it. Be modern. Put periods where they don't belong. Shorten words. Use LOL and OMG in your copy. start sentences with lowercase...use unnecessary ellipses (or even parentheticals). Use punctuation to change meaning. Play. The English language is not a stationary creature, it's an amorphous blob that you can mold and mess with. Have at it.

More words?
You've got to be kidding.

Body copy and other
longer form writing.

IT'S TRUE, NOBODY READS
YOUR COPY.

Somehow the lie has spread that people don't read anymore. Yet in a given day a person will read online news, blogs, twitter, instant messages, emails, signs, menus, presentations, online articles, to start. Then they go home to read a book and relax. At the very least they'll search through the descriptions of various shows. We read from morning to night. We probably read more than any generation on the planet, ever (take that, Renaissance). No matter what anybody tells you; words are here to stay. We have not and will not regress to hiero-glyphics on my watch.

What is true is that fewer people read poorly written ads. The standards have gone up quite a bit. The problem of course is that for the most part copywriters have not kept up. We're still writing in the same voices and styles as the 1950s. We have not given people a reason to read what we write.

Art directors are killing it. We're slack-ing. Come on people, let's do this!

A headline is interesting and engaging. It shocks you, stops you, makes you think. Body copy is no different. All too often body copy is treated as an explanation for the headline. This means either the headline isn't clear enough or the body copy is redundant. Neither is desirable for a stellar piece of communication.

A better way to think about the relationship between headline and body copy is as title and story. The title hints at what you're about to read, but doesn't tell it to you. *Romeo and Juliet* isn't called *Accidental Teen Love Suicides Because of a Series of Misunderstandings.*

Think of body copy as its own concept. Start over when you get to it. Write many paragraphs, just as you would headlines. Not just one. Sometimes you'll end up taking part of one paragraph and part of another. Sometimes you'll scrap them all because you think of a new direction. Sometimes one will just clearly be the winner. Maybe it'll even be the first one, but you'll never know unless you write a bunch.

The easiest way to pair body copy with headlines is to write the long copy part first and then go back and think of a headline that represents the theme of it.

It's bedtime but you're not tired. All you want to do is go outside and play flashlight tag with the neighbor kids. What could focus your mind away from all of the fun in your kid-life? A story.

A story is still one of the best ways to capture someone's attention. That's all we are as advertising creatives: storytellers.

Long copy is the purest form of this since it's close to a real novel page. You have the same tools as a classic writer. Even the approach and thinking is somewhat the same. Except the moral of any story you write will be to buy the product.

Conflict/Resolution:

This is very important for body copy. Your product must solve some problem, or be the resolution to some situation. The first part of this is to define the conflict. Sometimes the conflict is intuitive and you can set it up with just one word: "Termites." Other times it'll need more targeting: "Is it enough to eliminate most of your termites?"

Climax:

Build up to a single point in your copy. Have a distinct high point. It can be at the beginning or the end or anywhere else, but put it in there.

Visual language:

Make your reader see it. It's easier to re-member a picture of someone's face than a detailed written list of what someone looks like. Make people see your story and it'll stick with them for longer.

Characters:

You are not an ad guy talking, you are a character of the company. You don't have to create a fictional cartoon spokesperson for your product, or the story of some guy who founded the company. The characters don't have to be that close to the brand. In fact, the further away and more abstract they are the better the story can get. Though the further they are, the harder it is to connect them back to the selling message. Be careful.

You won't always define or introduce your character. You might just write from (or about) the character. For example, the Iliad didn't begin with Achilles saying "hi, I'm Achilles, I'm the best warrior ever. I don't like Troy."

Dialogue:

Just because you're not writing a script doesn't mean there can't be quotes. You can have a back and forth conversation with the reader. You can have a one-sided conversation. You can make your copy into a scene. You can answer your own rhetorical questions. Can't you?

Foreshadowing:

If your first line of copy hints at the end of it, then even if a reader doesn't finish reading, they get the gist.

Example of copy with story language:
Office supplies flew into the air, sent there by the blissful tornado that was Dave, standing triumphantly after his fantasy football victory. "Who's the man?" Dave inquired from his coworkers. But with a subscription to the latest football insights, delivered to his inbox daily, his coworkers in the league were all too aware of the answer.

Long-form advertising writing is a fairly unnatural process. You won't make a graph or an outline. You might eventually, but to start, you have an idea in mind and then you write until it appears on paper. I used to have trouble doing long copy because I'd get stuck in the structure of it, trying to land the ad perfectly from the very beginning. Logic and order come more in the editing than the writing. Treat long copy like a piece of documentary footage; you gather a bunch of content before you chop it together.

VERB A NOUN.

Hammer away.
Feather past.
Anchor in.

Nouns made into verbs are inherently visual. They play scenes in people's minds that make them harder to forget. They also come off as poetic, elegant, and thoughtful. It's instant character. It's one of the fastest ways to class up your language. Your CDs will cantaloupe.

START IN THE MIDDLE.

The beginning is usually all background and not altogether important. And if it is important, you can come back to it once people are interested. When you finish writing a block of copy, see if you can get rid of the first sentence. The first paragraph. All of it.

SPECIFIC IS MORE INTERESTING.

Getting specific is memorable for some reason. If I say I kicked you with my shoes it's less memorable than saying I kicked you in the shins with my purple high-tops. When a description is detailed it seems important. When you're reading a book and the author spends a page describing a character's face, you assume the character is vital, otherwise why would that much emphasis be put on them. Maybe this is trained into us as humans and we look for details. Whatever the reason, you'll get a better response from people if you get closer to the scene you're creating.

General:
Our new floral print dress.

Getting specific:
Our new floral print dress with flowers from the first blooms of springtime in Holland.

WIN THE ARGUMENT.
SELL A PRODUCT.

If a story doesn't seem right then consider a convincing argument. Go back to the Greeks on what makes arguments effective. There are three basic elements: Logos, Pathos, and Ethos.

LOGOS:
You're making sense for once.

Look, I know we all got into advertising because we didn't want real jobs, but sometimes you've got to roll up your sleeves and sink elbow deep into your product. Learn about it. Discover what is unique about it and why what is unique about it is unique. This is important on two levels, 1) it makes the work richer, 2) your clients will know you give a shit and let you get away with a lot more creatively.

If you can find beauty in the real facts about the product then you have struck gold. Your clients will do little happy dances around the conference table. Try not to make fun of them.

PATHOS:
Please, I just want to feel something. Anything.

Emotions are powerful. Just think of your last relationship. They can make us do what we ordinarily wouldn't. Emotions can infuse a product with a personality. Emotion finds a secret truth in a product that makes people fall in love with it. Emotion puts a finger on the pulse of a place and time. But, emotions are volatile. Use them wisely.

You can jump from heartfelt to angry, honest to sad, reflective to defensive. Pick emotions and jump around. Write the same ad with several feelings and see how drastically different they feel. Notice the change in pacing and language? Feelings are fun!

People want to be liked. Brands are no different. An important part of any campaign is finding a way for people to have faith in you. Convincing people that you're the guy to support. Apple is likeable and friendly. PC is cold and off-putting. Both are metal boxes with chips inside.

Said plainly:
A new kind of gin.

With an angry emotion:
Yeah it's a new kind of gin, what of it?

With an inspiring emotion:
It's a new day, and with it comes a gin.

Nothing makes a copywriter hate their job more than when they have to list multiple product benefits. It's gross and clunky. It's filled with impossible-to-pronounce words and names that have a handful of numbers in them like the Spoon4568B2. Just flows right off the tongue, doesn't it? Unfortunately, the days of the single-selling-point brief are gone. We have to work in a lot of junk.

In this type of copy you are bound to see world-changing phrases like "So that's why we…", "Introducing the first ever…", "no wonder…", "not anymore, because…" and a slew of other lifeless copy quips.

How can you write this type of copy in a way that both you and the world won't hate? There are a handful of approaches that can help.

Explain why a feature is the solution.

There has to be a problem or you can't fix it. Find the concern that is overcome by each of your product features and speak to them. Instead of saying an air purifier has an auto-dimmer, say it won't shine in your eyes at night.

Be poignant.

Find the human relevance in what you're being asked to say, because you're going to have to say it anyway. Find an honest narrative that readers can follow. If you're selling organic cereal, then you can talk about everything from the ingredients to happy employees through the lens of integrity.

Be brief.

Get it over with. There's only so much you can dance with a corpse before people get suspicious. If it's going to stand out no matter what, try not to linger.

Be consistent.

Are you saying "we" or "[COMPANY NAME]" or "I" or "they"? What scene are you in? Who are you as you talk? Anything is fine, but you will want to be consistent. Pick one and stick with it throughout the copy.

Pretty-up your vocab.

You're not going to win hearts with clichés. Find a more colorful way of saying the same point. There's a big difference between "comes with a 300-horsepower engine" and "armed with a 300-horsepower engine."

Talk to someone but don't pretend you know them.

The answer to "Have you ever thought/wondered/asked yourself_____?" is "No."

Use bullet points.

It'll break up the formatting and help differentiate what's important from what's listed information. It's also quicker to access in case there are 15 selling points to the product, but only a few that anyone would care about.

Be self aware.

Pull back the curtain. Admit that what you're talking about might be a handful. "The ZX4534AQ, a hard way to say something that will make your life simple."

Be honest.

If you know it's bullshit, everybody else will too. Try to find exactly how beneficial it is and say so. If you lie about or exaggerate the benefit, you will discredit any reasonable argument you might've made up to that point.

Be bigger.

In seeming contrast to the previous approach, you can make the benefit bigger than it is. Not by exaggerating, but by creating a true parallel. Rather than saying "it's the safest car ever" (a lie) you can say "a little safer is a lot when you're talking about your kid's life."

#1 rule:

IS THIS SOMETHING
YOU WOULD WANT TO
READ? IF YOU DON`T
WANT TO READ IT,
I DON`T EITHER.

TV or online video
or whatever it's called now.

The simple medium that people
love to make complicated.

YOU'RE THE BOSS AND
POWER FEELS SPLENDID.

Film is a management medium. You get the ball rolling in the right direction with a magnificent script, but there are so many people involved in the process that most of your work will be making sure others are doing their work. The people you choose can make a great idea OK and an OK idea great. This makes it both the easiest to do (no matter how complicated it gets, a script is no more than a few pages) and the most difficult (any person in the process can screw it up).

LUNCH IS ON THE CLIENT.
EAT YOUR WEIGHT IN REVENGE.

Being on production is like having a rich uncle. You live a lifestyle that is wholly inappropriate for your age and status. This, I imagine, is why it's often the most sought-after work by the senior people in an agency.

TV is the glamorous side of the industry. It's where you get to stay in nice hotels, eat fancy meals, and have production company staff laugh at your jokes that, honestly, aren't that funny. I'm sorry, they're just not.

Per unit, TV is still where most of your client's budget goes and thus where there's the most opportunity to scale up your idea. A small idea with a world-class director is still going to be pretty good.

TV is also the most openly critiqued face of the company. Before you're drinking champagne from bidets, create a script worth working on.

Ad time is relative, and 60 seconds for one project can feel like 6 seconds for another. Usually you'll be told exactly how long the commercial is that you have to work on. On occasion, it'll be up to you as the agency to recommend a length to the client. Though don't be surprised if you present a 60 and end up having to make 15s instead. The 30-second spot was once the industry standard when TV stations decided the length. Now the industry standard is 15 seconds with online media deciding the length. Commercials that people seek out on their own (unpaid media) tend to be 90-seconds to a few minutes. The industry overall is skewing shorter for the moment. But all this might change, so be ready to do them all.

YOU'VE GOT 60 SECONDS.

A 60-second commercial lets you build a connection with the viewer. You can bring them in close, take them on a journey, leave tasteful pauses, build a story arc. It's hard though to keep a viewer engaged for that long so don't get too into your pauses. It's a great length to change a viewer's emotional opinion of a brand, but doesn't generally do as well for pure awareness. You can skew awareness in your favor though with the "first five" rule. Make the product appear in the first five seconds of the commercial. Some entertainment brands even create mini-trailers that form the first five seconds of their longer commercial trailers.

The middle of the road, best/worst of both worlds. Enough time to introduce a simple story and have a few jokes or thoughtful moments. You won't have quite the emotional hit as a 60, but you can get people nodding and change some opinions. You can be charming and funny for sure, but heartfelt will get a little tougher. This is a great, hardworking length that won't cost a fortune to run.

Media companies love to tout 15s because statistically someone is more likely to watch a 15-second commercial all the way through than a 60 or 30. Because it's shorter, and that's how time works. This does well for pure awareness, but there's a good argument to be made that 15-second commercials don't do much to sway people or change their beliefs. It's not a lot of time to introduce a novel and compelling brand story and it's easy to fall into tropes because of it. You essentially have one scene to say everything you need to say.

One motion and a logo. Maybe you can squeeze in a headline. These spots also play without sound a lot of time. They are essentially print ads with a tiny bit of movement. And just when we all thought print was dead.

With a 30-second script you almost never go to more than one page. If the script is longer than that there's too much detail. If it's a 60 it's two pages tops. 15s are a half page. 6s are a couple lines. Beyond just taking less time to read, you can always ad-lib the description when you're presenting internally to CDs or clients and they won't hold you to some strange angle you promised in the script. A short and clean script will also prevent people from getting hung up on one small detail that was never that important to you in the first place. You never know when an entire script will be killed because the client doesn't like a reference you used that wasn't quite right to begin with. It goes beyond the agency and client too, the script will be a lot more attractive to a director if they can see that you'll let them put their mark on it. They'll kill themselves to do something amazing if they think the opportunity is there.

Aesthetics-wise, there is no universal "right look." Each creative director, client, or agency usually ends up with a favorite structure and style. Supposedly Jeff Goodby wants all of his scripts in Cochin 12pt. I don't know if this is true because I never sent him a script in any other format.

You'll usually get to see the most recent script done for a brand, or you can always ask for it from a CD or account person. Then copy the format. Generally, people won't get stressed about style as long as it's easy to follow, but it can't hurt to be consistent.

THE 31-SECOND SPOT:

When writing a script, give a lot of time for pauses, scene changes, and action. Everything takes longer than you'd think. Time it. Read the script slower than you want it read for the final and talk through visuals as you picture them happening. If it's a 30-second spot you end around 28 seconds. If it's 32 it will never fit into a 30. If it's 30 it will never fit into a 30.

Nobody will prep you for your first time on production. People will assume you already know what you're doing. If you're talented, you can trick people into thinking you do. Really, all anyone is waiting for is an opinion and a decision. Say you like it if you do, say you don't if it isn't quite right. Have an opinion and make sure it's one you can stick to. Think through your choices because nobody wants to redo everything every five seconds because of an indecisive creative. Be a leader.

It's up to you to get everything you want on film, in edit, in audio, everywhere. There will not be a chance to redo it.

Generally you won't have to push too much, but if you do, it's better to have people on set roll their eyes than your CD when you get back to the office.

This isn't the "trust yourself" speech. It's the "it's your ass" speech. Be stubborn, but kind. It's how winning work is made.

REWRITE
IN THE EDIT ROOM.

If you don't get what you want on film, it's amazing what editing can do. Pretend you're seeing the footage for the first time and create the best story the film offers. Maybe the ending you wrote isn't as funny as you thought it would be. Or the actor has a surprise limp that you didn't see in casting. Cut around your mistakes and nobody will know they were even there.

DON'T PANIC,
THEN SIT THERE QUIETLY.

Day one of your edit you will want to go to the top floor of the edit house and jump off the roof. Even if you're working with one of the best editors in the world you won't be happy with the first cut. I doubt it's ever happened that the first rough cut was what everyone hoped it would be. That's not the point though. The first edit is just to know that the footage does exist, that the scenes are all there and that if the world ended, something would be able to go on TV.

Now it's time for you and your editor to meld minds. Tell them what parts you think are working, what the overall spirit is you were going for, the pieces that didn't turn out the way you planned on the shoot. Give them your vision. Give a few notes of glaring mistakes or situations to avoid. Then sit back and let them work. I know I know, there are so many comments you still have. You could go on for an hour about what's not how you imagined. It'll get there, just don't give it all at once. If you are working with a great editor, sometimes the best use of your time at the edit is to say nothing.

Done right it should almost be a form of meditation. You breathe out some thoughts, the editor breathes it in and breathes out magic with it. That should be the flow of the conversation. If it starts to feel one sided and not like a meditative breath, you're doing it wrong.

Mind your manners too, your editor might have an Oscar or two. Also, pick up your dishes. You're a fucking grown-up and it'll change their perspective on you. Say thank you. Push in your chair when you go.

There's a misconception that the edit is a place where you simply glue the pieces of the spot together as you scripted it, add some spackle, and you're done. Editing is more like sculpting than building. You chip away, mold, squish around some squishy goop until it starts to look like what you want it to look like.

At first don't worry about the length. Just mash the pieces in the right place and see if it makes as much sense as it did when it was a script. It's not time yet to stress one exact take over another, just more or less make the spot understandable. It probably won't be, for a while. Start shifting around the big blocks of scenes. Watch it again, see if it makes sense, shift, watch it, panic, shift, then watch it again. If you shot what you scripted and then some, you should have more than enough material to make a good spot.

If it's a funny spot, the joke might not work yet, but that's ok, have faith.

Is it all working now? Ok, now worry about the length. Put it to the song you like, etc.

If you're not familiar with TV production, color-correction is the difference between an amateur video and a cinematic film. It's when the spot you worked on begins to look like a professional piece. The first basic step is making sure people don't look like they all have jaundice, seasickness, or sunburn—getting the greens, yellows, and reds all balanced. Also making sure white objects look white, black objects are black, etc. Of course the most important part is making sure the client's product is the 100% correct color (especially for food and beer). It's helpful to bring the product with you to the color correct session so they can see it in person. Any good post house can get you to this level before you even show up. Then comes the fun part, what story are you going to tell with color? The hipster Wes Anderson look is a push of a sepia yellow. A cold and sterile vibe is a touch of blue. Heartwarming is a warm color. It can get more or less serious with the saturation of color, even getting cartoonish if you push the saturation too far. Overly contrasted and crushed midtones gives you that classic ad look, pushed further it becomes a soap opera. The entire mood of a spot can change with what you do here. Find references you think are doing what you want to do. Work with the colorist to play and ask them lots and lots of questions. Most of them have worked on plenty of incredible feature films too and they have great opinions and taste.

DON'T PROMOTE OTHERS FOR FREE.

This is a dumb one, but make sure someone covers up any logos that aren't your brand's logo with tape on set. You'll either have to clear usage rights of every single brand that appears or blur it out in post-production. If you blur it in post you have to do a good job of it or it'll look like there are naughty parts everywhere, and that'll mean a ton of time wasted, especially if the logo is moving. It's not the end of the world by any means and they won't be strangers to doing it, it's just time and money that could be spent making the spot better.

GET READY TO HAVE A SONG IN YOUR HEAD FOREVER.

Life is better with a soundtrack. Just like music can change your mood, it can change the mood of a spot. Sometimes your whole idea for the spot will be based on a song. Other times you'll have some idea, but still be looking for the exact perfect track. Then there will be times you have no idea whatsoever. Start early, find references from your own music collection or online. Try watching the spot with different styles and genres first. Then once you've narrowed a category try to find specific songs or artists who seem to work, even if they're not in your budget. That's what you can cut your spot to as a guide for making sure the spot works. Then you can bring in a music house to help you make a bespoke track based on a general reference. You can leave it fairly open, "I'm looking for 25% Mozart, 75% Polka" or get specific, "I want something that sounds like this song but is different enough that we won't get sued."

If you let the client hear the scratch track be prepared for them to fall in love with it and either try to find a way to buy it or be heartbroken when they can't. Final warning: when you finally find the right song for your spot, you will have to hear it over and over and over again. But not even the whole song, just some 2-second segment that's over the part of the cut that's not working.

"Some part of the cu...the cut... 2-second...2 sec... part of...part of... part of the cut"

Animated spots are a weird wrinkle in the land of TV. You usually don't get to travel and they take just as much time and effort as a live-action spot. You'll have to give feedback in emails and the changes won't be made for hours or days. It's also tough to know what you're approving when. You'll hear a lot of words like storyboards, doughboys, lighting phase, etc. Ask the producer (and production company if you can) exactly what you're approving at each step. Loosely, a storyboard is going to be where you approve the framing and timing they're going for; pre-vis is where you see blobs showing you the movement, exact angles, and pacing of each scene (this is the last real time to change anything); then there will be a few more rounds of polish including color, shadows, and texture. Once each phase is locked, it's a massive pain in the ass to go back and change anything and you pretty much have to go all the way back to the beginning to tweak. You'll need client approval at each phase too, to avoid the headache of having to beg and plead the production company to change something you said would be fine.

If a scene feels off it's because it is off. If you reluctantly agree to a change, you'll regret it later. Trust other people's guts too, but be wary of logical explanations for errors. No person will be there to explain to every home viewer why it is the way it is.

When in doubt,
go with the Swedes.

Digital, social, and all of that.

More than any other medium, the guidelines for digital are a rapid work in progress. In general, it's a little looser, more casual, more entertaining. It pretty much has to be. With TV, people will put up with a commercial that's boring because they're too lazy to change the channel. With digital, they have to be motivated enough to become un-lazy and seek out your content. And it'd better be worth it or back they go to porn.

The copy for digital has to be simple and intuitive too or people will get lost and, well, back to porn. Strip away as much as you can. If you don't need a headline, don't put one. If the product name can be worked into the title, do that. Ditto for the logo. If you have a text box where people type, write the call-to-action in the box. Consolidate. Shrink. Chop off or mash together anything you can.

Go with clear over cute, but be very casual. Write like a blogger writes: informative but still engaging and light. The internet isn't a heavy medium, you will lose people with jargon. And if you lose them…you know.

The functionality is intuitive and quick, and it is easily accessible (you don't have to register, create a character from scratch, answer a quiz, etc.).

If you do for some reason have to enter information or upload a photo, it is asked in the most entertaining way possible and is well worth the hassle.

Nothing is more than three steps away.

I saw a site where the user was asked to register and answer a survey to discover what flavor of the product they're most like. Are you fucking kidding? Do they think I can't wait to post on my Facebook wall that I'm Raspberry-Razzle?

The bonus of being online is that you can dictate the parameters. Are 30 seconds not long enough for your commercial? Make it 37. Want more room for copy? Add a scroll bar. Headline too long? Have it come up in parts. Media restrictions are gone, all that's left to do is make it engaging. This freedom also makes it a bit unruly. Create your own boundaries early in the process so you have a way of checking your ideas.

REALITY IS THE FILTER.

Put yourself in the role of a first-time viewer. Does it still make sense? Is it worth the user's efforts? It's a bit foolish to assume people have seen other parts of the advertising campaign before they see the digital part. It's also naïve to assume that a regular person will go through tremendous lengths to receive your advertising messages.

The first part of doing something online is coming up with an idea. Just like anything else in advertising. If you jump straight to some neat new piece of technology you just heard about, it'll be outdated by the time the project goes live.

Think of what you want people to take away from the project, list them out. Then, think of ways you can group all of those ideas into one overarching digital idea. You also need to consider functional requirements.

Let's say you're working on a coffee brand that sells fair-trade beans. You want people to know about the people growing the beans, the importance of different regions, the different flavor profiles, etc. You might want to create an online campaign that tells all of these stories through the story of the growers.

There would be a page where you could get to know the growers and hear a personal story of how the company has impacted their lives in positive ways. On the product page you can learn about each bean variety as told by one farmer who grows it. The order page might tell you how much the farmer will get from that bag of beans. Each page achieves its own task, but builds up to the larger idea of the growers.

Figure out all your pieces, prioritize them, then find a way to put them together. There are infinite ways to weave them. Some will be more intuitive than others.

When you're doing a simple product like candy, soda, or anything else that doesn't require a lot of technical information, you'll want to keep your idea simple and easy to explore. With little new info, your purpose is entertainment—making people like you more than the other guy. What works best in this scenario is a single-experience. Ice Bucket Challenge, Elf-Yourself, Subservient Chicken, all of these had one, singular, simple experience that users could participate in and then move on. It's easy to share because you know what it is and can sum it up in a few words as you share it with your friends.

For a product launch or a complex product, you might have to get across a ton of information. The web allows you to do this in a classier way than TV or print. In a print ad you need to get all 14 product points into 8.5 x 11. On the web you have as many pages and sections as you want and you could have one page per product point if it felt right.

When you have a more elaborate product or project you will want to think a lot more about site structure. The idea of a single experience still holds true, but you won't have the luxury of one page. It's time to get organized.

Break out the sticky notes and a big board. Think structural, not linear.

Figure out how to break apart your site. Every product has natural seams to cut along. A car has drive, interior, safety, design. A washer has cleaning power, efficiency, clothes care. You can be somewhat avant-garde with it if you'd like, but find intuitive divisions and start putting all the information you have into each of those buckets. This will be your site structure.

You can then create a main page or an intro that ties them together. This landing page will house all information that is necessary to understanding what the heck to expect on the rest of the site.

Let's say for example that you are creating a site for a refrigerator, the concept is "the land of cold." The homepage will explain that it's a land of cold because otherwise when you get to the icicle monsters in the freezer section of the site, you will think "wtf! Icicle monsters?" Conversely, if the freezer section and the quick-cool section and the crisper drawer section all start off with "this is the land of cold," it will get very grating very fast.

BUILD A WORLD,
THEN LIVE IN IT.

MAKE DIGITAL
LESS DIGITAL

Unlike TV and print, which are confined to the media, a web experience exists wherever it wants to go. You can set your own guidelines, but once you do, make sure to follow them. If your tone is funny, it has to be funny from the banner to the Twitter to the About Us page. If the Instagram post is black and white, a sudden burst of color will be disturbing...is that what you were going for? If you have wacky green creatures walking through the site, a sudden serious page of copy will be out of place. The internet is a magic space where anything can happen, but if you jump the logic you've created, you will confuse or annoy people.

Working in the web means creating different stories and putting them under one roof. Each section or piece is a tale that is interesting on its own, but also should anchor to the main theme. An online narrative can be interrupted though, so make sure the story holds even if you skip steps. It has to make sense when it's out of order too.

Even though we're in a digital world, people still like touching, lifting, and poking. We want the instant convenience and accessibility of the digital world, but we're not ready to abandon the physical world. Some of the most intriguing digital experiences mimic the physical world or work on top of it. Tactile experiences like rolling or spinning or throwing will up time spent on the site. Giving weight and dimension will make objects more approachable and real. Using items and gestures that are instinctive makes it so you won't have to explain them.

I know to blow on a dandelion. I know to pick up dice. I know that if I spin a wheel it will eventually slow down and stop. If I drop an item, I know it falls. I don't know that clicking a box gives me a numerical value that relates to the image that will be selected on the orb in the upper right-hand corner.

The icky secret of how agencies make so many amazing digital experiences is that they don't. They hire other people to do the fine details. The idea comes from the agency along with much of the writing and the initial design, but then it gets handed off to one of many digital production companies. I've seen people make their careers by working with the right ones.

Search, study, and memorize a list of vendors you'd like to work with and what type of work they do. Anytime you see a cool project, find out who did it.

Finding the right people to work with is hard. Their site can be great and they can suck. They might be brilliant, but not brilliant for your project. They can be super smart, but impossible to work with. They can look amazing but the guy who did all their work has long since left and opened his or her own company. Ask lots of questions when you get on initial calls.

Then, once you've got a capable vendor, make sure to manage the project. Match your vision with their vision and the client's vision. You talk to the vendor through producers. Talk to your producer daily at least.

Digital and social media companies get delivered pillowcases filled with gold ingots for every project they do. There's no need to feel sorry for them unless they're not able to do what you're asking them to do because you're indecisive, slow, or wasting time.

Try and be as civil as possible, but tell them what you expect. Remember that you are nothing without them. You hired them because of your shortcomings, not theirs. You're partners. If they suck it's because you suck. If you guys do amazing work together it's at the very least partially because of them.

If they know what they're supposed to be doing but they don't, push them. One way you can make them nervous is to do some of the work yourself. Come up with solutions and tell them that's "a place to start." They'll raise it even further trying to one-up you. They'll also see that you give a shit and that'll make them care too.

They want you to be happy. A single bad experience can get a vendor blacklisted for years. A successful experience can mean a new level for their office.

Oh. And remember to say "thank you."

To date I have not been on a reasonable timeline for digital projects. By the time you get briefed you are behind the ball.

It's the best and worst part of it. Choose to focus on whichever aspect of it you'd like. On one hand it's stressful. On the other, it moves fast enough that it doesn't get ruined.

START WITH EVERYONE HATING YOU
AND GO FROM THERE.

Digital ads are the worst. You are in someone else's personal space. You aren't a bathroom break in their program, you are an open sore in their life. What's more, you're cheap and dirty, with the narrowest chance of being even remotely entertaining. An eye-tracking study found that people have been physically trained not to look where banners are placed. You're not even worth forgetting.

Step one is knowing that. Now you're ready to do digital.

STATIC OR SIMPLE ANIMATION ADS.
THE TINY THORNS.

These are the low-end of web. Because of the extreme size and space limitations there's very little you can do. Clients love them because they're cheap. Websites love them because they load super-fast so they don't screw up the main user experience. Creatives fucking hate them. If you're allowed some movement, and this goes for all digital ads to some extent, ensure the end frame makes sense on its own. You only get a few seconds of auto-play. Placing the message or an interaction at the end means that users have time to mess with it if they want to. If it's static, just think of it as a billboard or print ad, except that people can click instead of you needing to include all of the info right there.

RICH-MEDIA BANNERS:
AS PLEASANT AS SHIT CAN TASTE.

The term rich-media means you have way more options open to you. Get specifics, but you can assume you can do pictures, videos, experiences, and more. Rich-media also means there's a backend available where you can load in information (like local weather, traffic, or anything from a database). It's best to think of these as tiny interactive screens where anything can happen. Many rich-media units have become mini, low-budget TV spots. You have no audio unless people turn it on, plus people can interact, but it's TV.

When you're writing copy for banners or for Instagram/Facebook videos, or anywhere someone needs to read copy in a timed space, it still helps to time it out the way you hear it. If there's a pause before the punchline, have the punchline visually load after a pause. If you wonder how long a line should be up, read it aloud. That's how long. Timing is still everything. If the jokes hit at the right points it can lift a simple idea into a better idea.

Mindless digital ideas are some of the best digital ideas. They get the most engagement and a fair amount of click-through as well. Make it something you can fidget with, tap, or mouse over without thinking.

If you're not doing a brilliant execution that will change the world then go all the way down to dumb. Follow the "light as a feather" rule; if it's any more difficult than lifting a feather, most people won't do it.

...AND THEN THE AD INFLUENCES THE STUFF ON THE WEBPAGE!

You might think nobody has thought to do this, but they have. It's not original and it's a logistical nightmare getting the rights to all of the content on a page. Or you'll have to make fake content to fill the page and that's just stupid because it's still not that interesting. Plus, you're getting in the way of what people want to be looking at. Unless the thought is earth-changing, keep searching for the idea.

DEATH MAKES A CLICKING SOUND.

Ever since "punch the monkey," people have no faith that clicking won't take them away from their current page. If the ad requires a click or tap to engage, you will lose people. Try to make as much happen as possible without someone else needing to do something.

In the same realm, if your digital ad requires sound to work, you're kind of screwed. Most sites and apps won't allow sound without interaction or clicking, which, as previously stated, is death.

THE LEASH WE ALL
CARRY IN OUR POCKETS.

Apps make it into a lot of presentations but rarely into the real world. They are complicated, involve coding, and people have to choose to download them. Which means you then have to advertise the app. To which the client will think, "Hey! If you want to advertise something, how about the product I'm paying you to advertise?" Mobile is a great platform because more and more people look at it over anything else, and the ubiquity and functionality of it opens up tons of opportunities. But if you're making an app, it has to serve some brilliant, genuine utility or be such a great gimmick there's no way users won't download it. If you think of an idea that successfully does that, stop reading this, quit your job, and go make that. If not, you're better off finding ways to work within existing mobile platforms and channels.

INSTAGRAM, FACEBOOK, TWITTER, SNAPCHAT.
BY THE TIME YOU READ THIS, TWO OF THOSE
WILL SEEM LIKE I'M BEING FUNNY.

It's easy to think that a brand's goal with social media is to get lots of followers. Naturally, you'll want to repost cute and funny stories, just like your favorite influencer does. It works for them; it must work for you. You'll be tempted to think the brand tone is less important than being liked and talking like digital people talk. But people already have cool people to follow. They don't need a brand for that. It's infuriating to people when companies they're trusting with their hard-earned money talk like they're about to post a cover song on YouTube. Let the brand be the brand. Keep everything in the same brand voice you've worked so hard to cultivate across everything else. Find ways to be likable for being that.

Think of people with lots of followers as tiny little TV channels. They are great if they choose to talk about your product unprovoked, they're ok if you pay them to talk about your product in the context of what they do, they're robbing you if you're paying them to do what they'd do anyway because they're "influential."

Influencers can definitely give your brand a kick in the ass if you have compelling content that you want them to share, and they can be huge allies if they support a program you're doing, but they can also be bonfires of cash that would be better spent elsewhere. Think about where they fit into the grand scheme of the brand instead of using them as a crutch to relevancy.

Rather than try and use the latest features of whatever new social channel is in charge, think of general ideas that get people sharing. At least once a year you will be asked to come up with an idea that costs nothing but has the impact across social media of an atomic bomb. That'll be the whole brief. Just a "breakthrough" and "viral" idea about the brand. There will also be an idea done within the last year that every brief will point to that proves it can be done and that it's so simple. Just do the same thing as that one successful idea in a $220 billion industry that resonated despite all the odds and only cost $50k to make. It's statistically not that likely, but it does happen. The interesting fact about a lot of those big hit ideas is that they never come from a brief to make a big hit idea.

But it's not all up to chance. There are some general ways to know if something at least has the potential to go viral.

Here are a few of those ways:

It's for a good cause.

If it's doing good in the world, or at least talking about doing good in the world, more people are willing to put their cynicism on hold and share something. At least fewer people will outright shut it down.

It's controversial.

It's questionable, not universally loved, on the edge of social acceptability, or even a step too far. This one is tricky, because if you push it too much you might not like the attention it's getting. Ideally, you're just on that line where something is controversial enough to share, but not controversial enough that any reasonable person would actually be offended by it.

It's supported by a celebrity.

Famous people get photographed taking out the garbage, and garbage isn't that far off from most advertising. If the idea has a celebrity in it, it will get a certain base-level amount of attention. The less expected the role of the celebrity, the more views you can expect. An action star singing a love song will get more views than an action star in an action sequence in most cases.

METADATA IS…WAIT, KEEP READING, IT'S NOT BORING

There are two types of metadata: structural and descriptive. For the purposes of marketing you only need to worry about the descriptive part, the metatags. When you make a website, Google, Facebook, and co. would love if you provided some info about each page. It's basically what you want people to see when you appear in a search result: the search words you think you should be associated with, and the images and words that appear when people share you out to social pages. Metadata isn't visible on your site, but it's there when people are trying to find you. This is how most people will see you, if you have a successful viral campaign, and is the part of the conversation you can control.

Just like everything else in the age of new media, there's a battle between the engineers wanting the tech to be objective, the business side wanting to bring in sponsor dollars, and marketers trying to game the system to not have to pay those dollars as often as possible. Search is the first battlefield. Think like a person trying to find you. Not the words you think represent you, but instead the words you think your ideal target is most likely to search for, especially when looking for you. Are you unique enough and specific enough that you will be the only one to come up? The more common the words people search for, the less likely you'll pop up and the more likely you'll need to pay to stand out. The more common the words, the more expensive it gets. For example, if you're working for an organic juice company, you likely can't afford "organic" or "juice," but if they're the only juice company that uses some obscure rainforest fruit, you can put that fruit, or that fruit plus "organic," in the metadata and pay for Google search results on it. Or if the company has a unique and trademarked name that people will definitely search for, you can use that. It's actually a form of creative writing, except that the tone of voice is your customer and the scene is them doing Google searches.

Ads people climb inside of
and potentially sprain
their ankles on.

Experiential marketing beyond
a logo at a concert.

PLEASE TOUCH THE ADVERTISEMENTS.

Experiential marketing is any branding idea that people can physically touch, visit, or see in the real world. It includes events, installations, parties, performances, theaters, sampling, items, programs, and anything else that you can walk into or that lives outside of a paid media space. The key word in all of this that you might've missed is that it has to be a *branding* idea. A party with a logo is definitely an experience of sorts, but is it marketing? This chapter is about this old tool that is growing in popularity, with brands being smarter about what an experience can be and what it can make people feel.

BIG, SMALL, OR MULTIPLE.

There's something visually stunning about warped scale. A building is boring, but a shrunken building is interesting. A thumbtack is boring but a giant thumbtack is interesting. A piece of paper is boring, but a million pieces of paper are interesting. There's probably something to seeing exaggeration that reads as important to our monkey brains and makes us notice it. Regardless of the reason, it gives your mind a nice tickle and looks great in photos you share to social media.

Step-and-repeats are those backdrops you'll sometimes see at award shows that are covered in the logo of the event and the logos of all the sponsors. The intended basic premise is that you get your most influential guests to stand in front of it and take their photo. All with the hope that people will see the logos and get warm feelings about the brand because of it. This makes a lot of huge assumptions. One is that fans will seek out the photo in the first place. The people a brand wants to photograph are people who are photographed all the time. That means there are probably photos of them doing just about everything, including making out with somebody they shouldn't be. Which means the photo of them standing in front of a wall covered in logos is low on the list of photos people want to see. But their superfans might seek them out; you know, the ones that make dolls from their hair. Then you'd be making the second huge assumption, that this obsessed fan will look beyond the celebrity they're obsessed with, whose hair they have made a doll out of, and look to the wallpaper behind them with a magnifying glass and think, "Wow I love that brand for making a wall for people to stand in front of," while stroking their celebrity hair doll.

MAKE A GUEST LIST SO EXCLUSIVE YOU WOULDN'T BE ON IT.

A party is only as good as its guests. If there isn't a mechanism in place for invitations, nobody will show up to the party or take part in the program. You can work directly through a PR company, or you can go rogue and play the who-knows-who game in the office. You can also tap the client for their connections. There are three basic types of guests: 1) Paid guests: these are typically celebrities, people with draw, massive social presence, and throngs of people who follow them. They can be part of the reason press show up or they'll be their own press because of their number of followers. 2) Unpaid VIP guests: these are your influencers who have an interest in the theme of your experience as well as press whose job it is to write about your brand category—essentially people whose job it is to be there. 3) General public, the people who will set the vibe and fill the space with bodies and make the story authentic; they're the wild card in all of this. An experience needs the right mix of all three for the experience to be successful. If it's all celebs, the experience becomes about them instead of your product. If it's all influencers, then the experience has no heart and it'll come off as hollow and self-serving. If it's all general public, nobody outside of a small group of people will know it ever happened.

ALCOHOL IS THE GLUE THAT GETS YOUR GUESTS DRUNK.

The press likes to drink. Influencers like to drink. Most of your target audience will like to drink. If your event goes into the evening hours, people will be surprised if there's nothing to drink, and then they will leave to find booze. You'll also have to watch that you don't overserve people (technically it's a legal liability, but it's also just annoying) and if you have drinks you will also want to seriously consider food, even if it's just small bites. You'll want to absorb that booze so guests don't end up telling you how much they love you man, I mean really love you man. It's a sobriety test balancing act. One drunk person can ruin an entire night and trash what took you months to plan. A bunch of sober people can do just about as much damage. Simple rule: have booze if people are there for longer than an hour, have food if people are there with booze for longer than one hour.

The second you get access to the venue you will be using for an event or installation, get out some measuring tape and masking tape. Use the tape to map out the entire setup, at least based on your first instincts or to match any blueprints you've laid out. You'd be surprised how often this is the first time you discover issues, like doors that wouldn't open all the way because of an obstruction, or segments of floor that are crooked or warped to the point that you can't put anything on them. You'll also notice that the blueprints the venue gave you were way off and that the 10-foot wall is only 8 feet and 4 of those feet are in front of a fire exit that can't be used.

OH LOOK, ALL THE DETAILS THAT
FELL BETWEEN THE CRACKS.

Ask about bathrooms (1 for every 50 people minimum). Splurge for the nice toilets,
because people have a surprisingly good
memory when it comes to toilet quality and
cleanliness. Ask about air conditioning,
not just that they have it, but that it's strong
enough if the place is filled with hundreds
of people dancing (you might have to bring
in additional A/C). Mind the exits, because
even if your venue is enormous you might
not be allowed a lot of people because there
aren't enough exits. Don't plug anything
into an outlet unless your electrical person
says you can (you might overload and black-
out your entire venue because you didn't
know the delicate balance everything was
in), be nice to everyone because they'll save
your ass at some point. Think about the
line out front and what you'll do for people
who can't get in. Make sure nobody passes
out in the heat or freezes in the cold. Have a
VIP line, a General Admission line, and no
line at all for press because they should feel
special. Make sure somebody can manage
the different photographers/videographers
who will be on site at one time. If you don't
like something, change it. Lift with your legs.

Experiences are hundred-sided Rubik's Cubes and you're the hand turning them all. They're a puzzle made of guests, builders, artists, videographers, photographers, musicians, PR, caterers, cleaners, sound engineers, lighting tech, PAs, and security, at its simplest. You are the central point of opinion. If any of those pieces aren't in the right place it'll mess the rest up, so keep an eye and ear on everything. Get a walkie-talkie. Production companies who typically do events can handle a lot of this, but then you'll lose a bit of oversight. Stay involved in conversations, be interested, make decisions and communicate them to everyone who needs to know so there's no confusion.

No theater would ever open a play without a dress rehearsal. You won't want to open an event without one either. Invite friends and family, agency friends, people who want you to succeed. If it doesn't work with them, you're in trouble. Bring them all in and treat it as if it were an official day one. Ask people to tell you what they thought, look for mistakes, pressure test it, try to break it. If everything goes perfectly, you're lying to yourself. If your friends are all smiling and kind, then it went terribly awry and they're being polite. You can't possibly know what it's like until it's open so you can't possibly have thought of everything.

Even if your experience took place in the largest stadium in the world in Pyongyang, North Korea (which is not a good location for an event, just FYI), every seat filled, you'd still only physically reach 150,000 people. Which in straight reach in the advertising world is terrible. For reference, the 30-somethingth season of *Survivor* has around 8 million viewers per episode. What you don't get from TV is deep engagement and long-term interaction with the brand. You rarely, if ever, get notable people giving your TV commercial credibility, but you will with experiential. You'll also get press attention beyond the traditional advertising publications. There's a human interest in an experience that doesn't exist in traditional advertising. Get the right people there and you can have a two-hour conversation with them, changing the way they see the brand. If you can have powerful advocates, the rest will follow and you can have a major impact on brand perceptions.

You don't need to convince everyone on Earth, just the people who everyone on Earth look up to. If your favorite chef recommended a restaurant, you'd probably check it out. If a musician you love did a song with an artist you hadn't heard of, you'd listen to their album. If all your friends on Instagram went to the same event, even if you didn't make it, you'd think it was the place to be. In simplest terms, if the popular girl at school says it's cool, it's cool.

Pretend that on the day of your event everyone's cameras stopped working. Would there be any record that it ever happened? Would there be anything that you could share? What would you do if the news called up and asked for a clip? Is there something that the agency could share with future clients or that you could put on your own site to show off? Don't count on the press to show up with their own film equipment and get everything you need. You'll probably get photographers, but you'll also want video and a written storyline of the event, a narrative way to condense the entire event into an easily digestible snapshot. That way, no matter the format, you've got what you need to get noticed via 1) words, 2) photos, 3) video, 4) all of the above. Even before the event you'll want to get as much of this as possible. Get behind-the-scenes because you won't have another chance. You can't recreate an experience in post-production. Even if it's just an agency camera guy, or an intern with a video camera, make sure you get the build, the backstory, the production. If there's a huge line opening day, 100% get footage of it. Unlike with a TV spot where the behind-the-scenes is a huge wank fest, the behind-the-scenes of an experience is often an important part of the story.

BE A CREATIVE ARCHITECT.

Typically when you write in advertising, it's narrative and linear. In experience work you will write in structural building blocks. What's the smallest and simplest the message can be and still make sense, what's the longest and most informative it can be while still being readable and interesting? You'll be writing for everything from pins to 30-foot walls. Bathroom signs will need copy as will social media posts. Press releases will need synopses and news sites will need quotes. Create a phrase that's your elevator pitch for why someone should care about the idea, write a paragraph that's your phrase plus the most interesting parts of the idea, then create a page that starts with that paragraph and then gets into all of the details and an alternate version that also includes the client/brand benefit. That's your basic kit of parts that you can tweak slightly for each individual need and will save you hours of stress later.

A ROSE BY ANOTHER NAME IS THE GREAT RED
FLOWER 4000.

Coming up with a name for your experiential idea is as important as naming a
product. It's the shorthand everyone will
use both internally and externally to pitch
the idea. It's the name the client will say in
the lunchroom to impress their coworkers.
It's the name you'll have to say 100 times
to vendors and partners. It's also the way
the press will introduce it to the world and
will likely be your hashtag. One good way
to come up with a name is to think of it as
a one or two-word headline. Look into the
brand's DNA and the experience idea itself
and think of words that overlap between the
two. Make the name telegraphic and clear
as to what the idea is. Think of words that
toy with the idea, exaggerating or under-
playing it. If it's huge, consider calling it
tiny. Be descriptive and use the language
and tone of your creation. If it's a house is it
a manor, estate, shack, home, or mansion?
Is the name friendly and approachable or
staggering and awe-inspiring? If there's no
perfect word consider making one up, or
mashing up two words. Use roots of words
and all those Latin word origins to get
across what you're going for. Once you've
got something you like, say it out loud to
a bunch of people. If it makes you cringe,
keep going.

Somebody within the organization will be all about numbers, and you can argue the merits of deep conversations all you want or you can cook the books in your favor. When you do an experience there's a certain amount of basic sharing you can expect simply because some people share every moment of their lives. Beyond that, there are three different categories of sharing that you can use to keep the numbers up. The first is the dumb one. Simply pay influencers to show up and post. You can guarantee their reach and require them to make a certain number of posts over a set period of time. The best part is that you can often pull this from the client's media budget so it doesn't take away from your production. The second way is building in sharable interactions. The simplest version of this is a photo booth that shares right to somebody's social media. You can get more creative than that too with overlays, distortions, candid images, props, or building them into unexpected places like scanners. Maybe it's not a photo at all, maybe it captures something they create or it's a video or an animation of the guest. You get the idea. Basically, since it's in the space people will interact with it because they'll feel they should. Otherwise they'll fear they missed out. The third way to get people to share is to give them that iconic moment that they feel compelled to take a photo of. At a wedding it's the first kiss. At a concert it's the encore. It can be a central sculpture or a noted time or a moment. It can be an extremely personalized moment or a huge public spectacle. You'll know it's a success if two seconds after it everybody is staring at their phones to make sure it posted. Last note, imagine thousands of people in a small space all using the same signal at exactly the same moment. You've got to have some amazing Wi-Fi and it'll have to be open network. You'd hate to lose all that sharing due to a poor connection.

What makes a fun event:
Good people, good drink,
good music, something to
take a picture of.

HIGH ON HASHTAGS.

It's usually tasteless to make brand icons huge, especially a hashtag or a logo, but experiences are the one instance where I wouldn't say that's the case. Make it enormous. Gaudy huge. At least double what would seem excessive in ordinary circumstances. Because once you fill the venue with hundreds of people, dim the lights, turn on the smoke machine, blast wall-shaking music, you will barely be able to see it. It will feel hidden unless it's gigantic and high enough that nobody could block it. Also, and this is rare in advertising, people will actually be looking for it. They want to know what hashtag to use to make sure everyone knows they were there. If people want to share the brand, who are you to deny them?

DID YOU HEAR ABOUT THAT PARTY NOBODY HEARD ABOUT?

One of the quirks of experiences is that they are part ad and part something that needs to be advertised. "Foot traffic" as the sole way people find out about what you've created is the same as posting a video to your Facebook friends and hoping it goes viral. There's a chance, sure, but not a good one. Hand out flyers, make posters, billboards, get posted in the local blogs, send out invites to people of interest, post teaser videos. Promote until your invite list is at least 50% OVER total capacity. Expect at least half of people not to show up in a best case scenario.

If your experience is something people can walk into, a physical space of some form, you'll need to fill it with programming. It could be bands performing, artists painting, creative people performing in any other way, whatever. The space itself can be inspiring, but it'll get boring and each new program in the space is another reason someone can have to write about it and visit it. It's another audience who can find out about it and another list of potential guests who will make the effort to show up. The program ideally matches the ambition and narrative of your space, so it doesn't overshadow the event itself or underwhelm people by comparison, or come out of nowhere. A good measure is the photo-moment test. If the programming becomes more iconic than the experience, you've just created a set for someone else's brand.

Goodbye, nights
and weekends.

Pitching new business.

NOT JUST FOR MAKING
YOUR BOSSES RICHER.

The saying goes that the first day you work on a piece of business is the first day you begin to lose it. That means they'll have to lay off you and your friends if they don't have something to replace it with soon. Even if agencies don't lose business, it's still important for an agency to be able to expand its stage. A boss of mine once put it like this: talented people want to grow and if the agency doesn't give them the space to grow into, the talented people will leave. Pitching new business is a necessary evil in that quest for growth. A quest you will periodically be brought along on whether you like it or not. Here's a bit of what to expect: A pitch is like a reality TV dating show where agencies compete against one another to court clients by showing that their ads are smarter, more creative, and more interesting, and hoping the client doesn't just pick the hot agency because they're hot.

Every now and then you can come in with an idea so brilliant that they throw caution to the wind and make out with your agency, and it feels so damned good. Through the process you will have great bonding moments with your colleagues, because you are deep in the trenches together, late into the night, with agency top brass paying close attention and making lots of eye contact with you. It's a rare occasion where the best idea can truly come from anywhere—because money. Get ready for long hours and frustration, but also laughter and good old-fashioned human connection. It's a perfect place to make a name for yourself, make some new friends, and pick up some weird stories from when you all lose your minds around 3 a.m. It can be a lot of fun, if it doesn't kill you.

If you're on a pitch, almost for sure you're not going to produce a single thing that you presented in the meeting. If anything does get made it will be the manifesto video you showed to sell the idea, but you never imagined would be seen by a single consumer (more on that later). It seems a shame, but it's freeing as well. You don't have to hold back. You don't have to worry about logistics or directors or any of that. You just have to think in the broadest possible perspective, without any taint or skew from past experiences. You're the step before the first date, just thinking of that one line that'll start a longer conversation.

LIKE SMART,
BUT SIMPLER.

To win a pitch, keep ideas brief. If any idea takes longer than 15 seconds to explain, kill it. No matter how genius it is. You can show it later if you actually win the business. Repeat your one hero line forever. Put it on everything. Win through consistency. If you have an outlier, kill it. They're not buying ads, they're buying a vision and the clearer the vision the more likely they are to buy it. You can change it later, edit it, etc. As previously mentioned, you won't be making any of it anyway. You just need a big idea, and by big idea I mean you need one idea. A single breakthrough insight brought to life over and over again until you can't miss it. A thought so all-encompassing that you can quickly spit out 100 pages of ideas, because you'll need 100 pages of ideas, and you've got about 2 weeks to do it. Think wide instead of deep. When the client is making a decision they need to know exactly what you showed them and what they're buying if they choose you.

WHAT'S A MANIFESTO?
IT SOUNDS IMPORTANT.

I never used the word manifesto before I got into advertising and now it's one of the biggest parts of my job. It's the lead page in any campaign presentation and especially for a pitch presentation. It can take the form of words center-aligned on a colored background, words across several pages paired with (juxtaposed or literal) visuals, or a video with those words read in a folksy, witty, or British-sounding voice. A manifesto is a string of about 15-20 lines that in sum makes anyone who reads it viscerally and intellectually understand a brand platform and tone. It can be funny or serious. It can be a vibe or a logical progression. It can be emotional or blasé. The easy way to get to a manifesto is: intriguing thought at the beginning (a truth or a question), a line at the end that could maybe be mistaken for a tagline (even if it's just a tagline for the next hour), fill in the rest of the manifesto with language that flows from your insight to the line at the end. You can do this with examples or repetition (always in threes, because thoughts sound better in threes). You can do this with more questions that start from your first question. You can do this with almost random sentences that feel in the same tone, as if you're just an observer hearing those phrases coming from the brand. There should be a bit of an arc, leading you along a journey to your final closing insight. It'll take some practice, but once you get the hang of it you'll be able to communicate with a client quickly and save having to explain every idea for 15 minutes.

The idiot-proof manifesto is this:
"Blah used to be great, but then blank happened. Shit started to suck, we lost our way and/or times changed. But now there's product. Changing the way/getting us back to the way we blah. Because in today's world we need more blah. Product—cleverline."

You'll probably hear the term "pitch theater" when you first work on a pitch. No need to buy clown makeup, all pitch theater means is having one special something you can bring to the meeting that isn't an ad, but that will make the clients like you. Because, as important as the work is, the potential client is also thinking, "these are the people I have to meet with every day for the next few years."

The difference between a quick and clever pitch theater idea and a cheesy idea often comes down to context and execution. If the meeting takes place at the client's offices, tone it way back. We sometimes forget that agency offices are places where dreams and silliness are not only welcome, but encouraged. Even stodgy agencies. But corporations don't usually inspire the same spirit. A good test of your idea is to think if it would still be clever if you were presenting it in a noisy food court and you had to stop for a minute halfway through presenting it. If you're presenting it in your own office, you've got a lot more leeway. Then, make sure it's executed fully, not cheaply. If your pitch theater feels flimsy, it'll come off as pandering or as a gimmick. Lastly, if the meeting is going well, clients will love this stuff. If they're not feeling the work, they won't. It's either the cherry on top or the coffin nail, with little in between. If the work is great, feel free to skip it and just be memorable in the way you present.

If you're pitching a chain of butcher shops, you might wrap the presentation in high-quality butcher paper, tied elegantly with twine, a perfectly typeset sticker on it featuring the butcher shop's name and the name of the agency. Done tastefully it'll look thoughtful. Done poorly it'll look like you put five cents worth of brown paper around their multimillion-dollar brand.

If you're pitching a furniture brand, maybe the team assembles all the furniture that will be used in the meeting and films a time-lapse of it, showing this film at the end of the meeting to the surprise of the prospective clients.

Losing a month's work
in five seconds.

The delicate art of presenting.

Your ad is a Fabergé egg rolling through a minefield. Students just make ads good. Professionals make ads good, then watch them die for no reason, and then do it again as if nothing happened.

I have a TV spot that's fully-produced, color-corrected, cost the client $300,000, and has yet to air. It's mind-boggling.

Be prepared for some heartbreak, but also know that smart work does get produced. And, all this craziness is what makes it feel special when it does. Keep hope alive.

A friend and one of the few people with two black D&AD pencils, had this to say: "Good work has to get produced. I've just gotta believe that." It seems to have worked for her.

The following are real reasons an idea has died

Too funny. Not funny enough. The product no longer exists. There's no money. The suppliers don't like it. We can't find a vendor. We don't have the media space for it. Someone sent a complaint letter so the whole campaign died. The client showed it to a friend who has an English minor and they think that the writing isn't good. The focus groups don't like it. The focus groups like it, but people in the focus group worry that others might not like it. Too colloquial. Not colloquial enough. Too expensive to produce. Not enough time. It's not the right time. There's something similar to it. It's too new. It would work if it were Spanish. The CD doesn't like it. The client doesn't like it. The client is worried their boss won't like it. The client's boss doesn't like it. The client's boss doesn't like the client. The account left. The client doesn't want unicorns because they're extinct and we don't want to remind people of it.

Above anything else, keep in mind that your ad must be the missing piece of the sell puzzle. Explain how your work does that and the ad will be on its way.

If that doesn't work, find out what your client's real concern is. Sometimes it's as human as not wanting to get yelled at by their boss. If you offer to arm them with case studies, references, etc., then they might bite on work that's juicier than you thought they would.

EVERYONE IS DOING THEIR JOB.
YOU DO YOURS.

The client wants to sign off on an idea eventually, the account team wants to sell something that makes the client happy, and your creative director wants to sell either your idea or the other idea from the other team. Basically, it's on you if you want your idea sold. You might want to blame the account team or the creative directors or the planners or anybody else if the work dies. If you're in the meeting, it's on you to know how to sell.

Beyond my advice here I recommend reading some serious books on sales. I also suggest watching the best creatives in your agency in action. Some people are sell artists and it's stunning to see them do their art. I remember sitting in a meeting with one of my creative directors and lifting my jaw off the table as he turned the client around 180° from hating an idea to signing off on it because she loved it. He understood her concerns and was able to talk it through until they realized that they both did and didn't want the same aspects of the execution. It was magic.

In your first few years you're going to blow a lot of meetings. If you have quality bosses, they'll let you. Then, slowly, you'll notice that you are selling work that you thought had no chance. You'll think the client is just having a good day until you see them bite someone else's head off a minute later. It's just you.

CLIENTS ARE PEOPLE.
LIKE, THE HUMAN KIND.

Not just people, oftentimes very intelligent people. They've managed to work their way into trusted positions within a company through many years of hard work. And they don't want it taken away from them by some hot-headed twenty-something from art school who thinks this or that would be funny. Have this in mind any time you present to them. They are not impressed with your awards from competitions they've never heard of (they probably have their own from competitions you've never heard of), they want you to tell them an insight that they didn't know in a way that they can believe.

In reality, clients would ease up if they had any idea how much time and thought went into every piece of communication we create. If they knew that a dozen conversations at three levels of the organization occurred before arriving at 13pt italics. Let the client into your thinking a bit and give them a tour of the process. It's easier to buy work when you know it's thoughtful.

TAKE A BREATH.

I do it before writing. I do it before walking in the CD's office. I do it before presenting to a client. It's simple. It works.

TALK. SLOWLY.

It's nice that you're excited about the work you're presenting, but if you start talking a mile a minute you might come off as panicked and insecure. Take your time. No need to rush it. Let the client appreciate the work that you put so much time into. Let them hear every word so they understand you. Be loving about it. Treat your work with tenderness and familiarity, even if you just wrote it an hour ago.

KEEP THE MEETING MOVING.

If the meeting's going great, keep it moving. If the meeting's going terribly, keep it moving. The meeting is for selling work and getting clarification. If you're not doing one of those two, hit the mute button and say, "can we keep this moving?" Or do it yourself if you're in charge. Nothing positive can come of dead air.

When there's a long pause, the natural human instinct is to try and fill it. Since the client generally talks in comments, they will fill the dead air with comments.

DON'T WAKE THE DEAD.

If an idea has died, you don't want the client to dwell on it. I've been in two-hour meetings where all we did was kill one idea. It's dead, leave it be.

If a client tells you they don't like some aspect, take notes on what they don't like, tell them you'll look at ways to resolve it, and move on. Present it. Try to push it through once. If there's still resistance you say "ok, we understand your concerns, let us look back at it." There is no use lingering. They don't like it. Step away and re-examine the idea to see if there's a delicate way to fix it to the client's liking and yours. It's amazing how small the compromises are that they expect from you if you're willing to listen to their concerns. But that's for you to do on your time, not during the meeting. If you turn it into a pissing match right there, they'll win. They have the money.

This is the flipside of not selling work enough. I've seen this too many times and I've done this personally an uncomfortable number of times. You're in a presentation, the client loves what you're putting out there. They even tell you so. It's sold!

Then, you keep going...

You tell them about this brilliant intricacy of the idea that they might've missed. They agree. The subtlety of the gradient you used. They love it. Then of how great the photographer is that you referenced. Then, before you know it, the client has decided that they don't love it anymore because they didn't realize that you were referencing a photographer who was popular in the 80s and it doesn't feel modern enough for what they are going for. You just over-sold the idea.

SING TOGETHER.

You know when DJs switch songs in the middle of a phrase and it doesn't quite work with the next song but they act like it does? That's what it sounds like when two creatives are trying to sell an idea. Pick a person BEFORE the meeting who will lead the call. Then, the other person only comes in when directly asked a question or in dire circumstances where only they can save the call.

POLLY WANTS TO SELL CRACKERS.

Try not to parrot other presenters in the meeting. People love to put in their reframing and rephrasing of what was just said because they're certain their way is more eloquent. Especially if they're trying to convince the client of a point. It's been said, why be redundant? It slows the meeting, undermines the credibility of your partners, and makes you sound like an ass. It also gives a second chance for the client to find something to object to.

BE "SMART."

There's a lesson I learned from a creative director early in my career that has served me well. Don't use the word "cool" to describe an idea. Use the word "smart" instead. This semantic switch can have a huge effect. Why? Because when you tell a client an idea is "cool" a voice in their head answers, "you know what'd be cool? If you moved some fucking product!"

PUT A LITTLE THEATER INTO IT.

Give the client a show they can't forget and maybe they won't forget you. They know you're not just talking as friends, they know you're there to sell them an ad. Why not lay into it? Be super heartfelt. Be funny and charming. Be playful and childlike. If it's about the work then you're just there for show. Your meeting will go better if they like the channel.

MAKE ROOM FOR MAYBE.

Try to sneak your favorite idea in as an option to keep on the table. You don't have to get the client to commit to doing it, just to letting you explore it more. It gives a bit more time for them to warm to it and for you to customize it to match the client's needs. Even the craziest ideas look less shocking the second time around.

Slick salesmen aren't slick salesmen. The best way to talk to a client is with truth.

I was in an important client meeting and gave some BS reason why we didn't add a tagline to a billboard (something about it being confusing on the same ad with another line). The client accepted the reasoning and we flipped to the next ad in the campaign. It had the tagline on it. The client asked why this one was any different. I started to say a reason, stopped myself and said, "sorry, I made that up. We just thought it was ugly." The client laughed and we sold the work.

If you think a line would be ugly, why would you say it doesn't work strategically? Just tell them it'd be ugly. Right around this time the account team will try and jump in and save the meeting because they're afraid the client will be shocked with how blunt you are. Chances are the client will be thrilled that somebody told them what they think. If they want it changed, they'll change it anyway.

Words of wisdom.
Or at the very least,
words.

Hard lessons of unfortunate origin.

MAKE
MISTAKES.

I want these two words art directed by somebody who knows how to art direct and placed above my desk in huge letters. This whole book is about the right way to do advertising, but making mistakes is more important to the process. Please let yourself screw up. Allow yourself to do work that seems wrong, obscure, or questionable. And if you do bad work on accident, let it go. It's pointless to beat yourself up over doing bad work, because everybody does bad work sometimes. I could show you ads I've done that would make you burn the rest of this book. I've learned that the important thing isn't to be flawless, it's to keep going.

DON'T WAIT FOR SOMEONE ELSE TO DECIDE IT'S TIME FOR YOUR CAREER TO START.

If you aren't getting briefs, make them up. If you get a shitty brief, find the most twisted possible way to interpret it. Or rewrite it. If you get assigned the small part, add the big part yourself.

There's a standard progression at every company and it's not a path you want to go down. It's a path through the crack neighborhood of mediocrity. Nobody is happy and there's lots of busy work.

In some ways your first day at an agency is when you have the most opportunity. Nobody has bogged you down with the work that pays the bills.

One weekend my AD and I had a random idea for a brand that we had never worked on. We did a simple little comp and brought it to Jeff Goodby. He said "That's funny. Do it." And so we did.

If we'd gone the proper route, we would've had two planners, two levels of account people, and two creative directors who'd have to approve it before Jeff would see it. It was off-strategy, unrelated to the campaign, and unbriefed. What do you think the chances are it would've made it up the chain?

If you want to create groundbreaking ads that you weren't assigned, aim high. The partners want you to present work without invitation, and they can sell it too. You might bruise a few egos along the way, but this is a route that for sure works.

THERE'S NO AWARD-WINNING AGENCY.

Bricks don't make ads, the people do. Superstar agencies hire you because they like your work. Then they give you a crappy assignment and wait for you to sprinkle your fairy dust. Making memorable work is your problem, not theirs.

Even at the best agencies in the world, there are only a handful of choice assignments per year.

There was a time when I complained about not getting assigned what I wanted, but there are people who whine way better than I do. Senior whiners. At a great shop there's a long line of talented people and not enough fun work to go around. I can count the number of amazing briefs I've been assigned on one hand, even if you cut three of my fingers off.

WEASEL IN ANY WAY YOU CAN.

Get in. Figure the rest out later. This applies to both agencies and projects. It doesn't matter how low you come in, look at who you're working for and what brand you're working on more than the specific assignment or place. My first full-sized, big-budget, huge opportunity website I got to work on because I did an auto-show brochure. When the website came around I was the only one who knew enough about the car to do it.

Point being, one assignment grows into the next, grows into the next, grows into the next. Nail that first one and it'll grow into bigger and better opportunities. Screw it up and it'll grow into a crappy time-suck. Either way, each new assignment is just one track; if it fizzles out, start a new one.

When your CDs are working on highly scrutinized TV spots, they couldn't care less about your teensy little project. Same with the client since it's a small budget and their boss isn't paying attention either.

This is perfect. Nobody is looking. This is your chance to do what you want to do. Show off why they hired you. If you care when others are scrambling, they'll let you take the reins. Then it'll grow so big that they can't control it and it's too late, mwahahaha!

Most awards are won on projects that nobody expected to be impressive. The little ones are the best ones. Nurture them.

It's hard not to feel dejected when a CD doesn't like an ad you did. Especially when they're right. Isn't it nice to know that the people above you are more talented? They know you're just starting off on your journey, they're not thinking you're an idiot. They want you to learn because they want to have another creative they can trust. Take the lesson. Leave the frustration.

SOME BRIEFS
YOU CAN'T SALVAGE.

I hate saying this, I do, but some briefs are just bad. It has less to do with the piece of paper with the brief on it and more to do with the people managing the work. If the Associate Creative Director keeps you from talking to the CDs, if the account teams keep you from getting feedback directly, if the work is filtered through 14 layers of people, you won't have the same chance to get work through. Push against the wall and see if it budges. If it doesn't, try to go around it.

If there's no hope, do the work with as much grace and speed as possible. You know the joke of the two guys running from a bear and one says, "you know this is futile, we can't outrun a bear," and the other says "I don't have to outrun the bear, just you." It's kind of like that. Do your work just slightly better than the team before you and you can keep the bear away. You won't be fired for doing better work, and you won't kill yourself on a lost cause either.

As a starting creative your raises come almost exclusively on the fame of your work. If you do work that gets attention and wins awards you get better projects. If you don't, you won't. If you increase your clients' sales, it doesn't affect your salary one dollar. Your success is not tied to the brand's early on. It's silly, but that's just the truth.

Why then should you care about doing work that increases profits? Because that's your job. Who wants to live in a world where a surgeon is rich and famous for their technique but kills all of their patients?

If one direction changes, move in the other with full steam. If the idea is approved, immediately push it beyond what was approved. If it's in production, try and capture an alternate option.

Imagine you're a shark and if you stop moving you'll die. It's not far from the truth.

RIPE FRUIT
ROTS.

As soon as your idea gets some traction, get it sold and out the door. Move immediately into production. Sign people on that week if you can. Get a director quickly. The less time between start and finish the better your idea will be in the end. The longer it takes the more chances it has to either die or be "improved" by someone or other.

NOBODY KNOWS OR CARES
WHO YOU ARE.

When you first come into a big-shot agency there will be a lot of trickle-down work for you to do. It won't be thinking about big campaign ideas or writing the next Super Bowl spot. It will be doing the 5-second button that starts with "brought to you by..."

Everyone has big ideas. They hired you because you have big ideas. They also hired your award-winning boss who's been doing ads for 20 years because he/she has big ideas. Thus he/she will be the one thinking of big ideas for you to work on. What is requested of you for now is craft. Look at your title, does it say copywriter? Art director? Shockingly, that's what you're expected to know how to do.

Charles comes back from Cannes and is getting praise and high-fives from just about everyone in the office. The Pope makes a special surprise visit to congratulate him. You, on the other hand, are working on a banner. You want the subhead to say, "It's all about the quality" instead of "It's all about the quality of the products we make."

Your battle seems stupid. Small. Insignificant.

Fight the fight. Make the ad just a little better. Then, once that line is where you want it, work on the next line. Every day, every moment you're on it, make it a little better. Savor those small wins. Celebrate even if it's by yourself. If you can find one part in every ad you do that makes you giggle, you will find that rarest joy: the ability to be happy with your job.

One of my favorite writings I've done is the legal copy on a banner ad. It's friggin' hilarious, but nobody other than me and maybe one lawyer will ever see it. It still makes me proud.

You`ll be fine.
Or not.

Counterintuitive inspiration on
being an advertising creative.

Not worrying about how impressive you are is freeing. In the industry there is only one Jeff Goodby, one Susan Hoffman, one David Droga. There are only a dozen or so name-brand creative directors in the whole world. Statistically the chances of being one of them is slim. If you are one of them, you'll rise no matter what. The most talented people I know have no idea how talented they are, they just do their work. It's better to think about how to make the work better than to try and convince people, including yourself, of how great you are.

YOU ARE BETTER THAN
YOU'RE CAPABLE OF BEING.

An agency partner once joked that if it weren't for people depending on him he would just sit on his couch drinking beer all day.

If you let the people around you lift you, influence you, inspire you then you will find yourself doing work you didn't know you could do. Put the ego aside and let the team infect your work.

Award shows are proof that focus groups, even with bright individuals, have little ability to judge work. The truth is, any one brilliant creative director saying they like my ad means more than a brilliant creative director and a handful of people I don't know coming to a consensus that my ad is worthy. If you're looking for a measure of success outside of the agency, see how many people write and talk about your ad. If nobody does, no judge in the world can give it value.

Every project starts somewhere. There are lots of a-little-bit-betters that go into making an ad amazing. Forward progress is the most important goal. Steady improvement. You'll have many rounds before an idea will be final and if you aim to push it a bit every time it comes back to you, you will end up with a great end result. If instead you try and start with "perfect" you will waste time, miss deadlines, and be so bitter when an idea changes that you will have trouble finding the want to get up and start again. Plus, in the end, your perfect and precious ad will not be as polished as the one that has been improved consistently.

If you're capable, you hold yourself to a high standard naturally. Others around you will as well. If on top of that you stress to the point of exhaustion, you won't be improving the work, you'll be burnt-out in a year and you won't see or enjoy the real opportunities. I learned this lesson late and hard. I hope you don't.

YOU'RE A TOTAL HACK
SOMETIMES.

The best advice I've gotten about having an off day came from a pair of CDs I respected a great deal, but just couldn't impress. A week into a project under these guys, my art director and I couldn't think of a single idea worth presenting. We were freaking out. We apologized. This is what they said:

"It's just part of being in advertising. It happens. Don't worry about it. Or actually, do worry about it. Worry about it a lot, because that's part of it too. Just know that you will get over it at some point and you'll get back to doing good stuff. Just hang in there and keep going."

Unless a super villain has requested that you create an ad that will convince him to put down the detonator, you're just making an ad. No matter how great or how bad, it won't make or break the world, your life, or even your career. Relax. Have fun. Even if it is a big deal you'll do better work if you take it lightly. If you wanted a serious job you'd go be a doctor.

For better or worse, advertising is more than a job. It consumes you. It wears you out and it makes you happy. Occasionally even in love. Tell me you've never gotten that sparkly euphoric feeling when you've cracked a problem. Tell me that and I'll tell you you're in the wrong field.

We're messed up as creatives, because it does matter to us. And because of that it is important.

Ads or not, we're leaving a tangible legacy. People quote commercials in hallways and hum jingles when they're in shopping aisles. Everyone remembers ads from when they were growing up. We're creating something that lives on. Why not make it worth keeping around?

If you are a human then you can be overworked, overstressed, and over-stretched. Most of you will learn this unpleasantly. I used to think I could never get tired. Never get burnt-out. Never get anxiety over my job. Never drop the ball. That was false. You can. You will. It's not the end of the world, just take a day off, sit in a café, read a book, and lick your wounds. Go easy on yourself. It's OK. You're human.

At the end of the day you are not going to be serving communities for the joy of philanthropy. You will be selling products to people. People who like to buy name brands. Name brands that you're trying to create. Deal with it. You will make yourself miserable if you think you're above everyone else in your ranks. You are no less evil than your clients in the grand scheme.

Actually, they do more for humanity since they leave work on time to coach their kid's Little League. Nope, you are a monster. You work for the man. You are the man. Know that and maybe you can do work for not just your client, but society.

Lie to yourself. Build it up. Make it more important than it is. Inspire yourself any way that you can to do better work. "Guys, this is it," is a phrase you'll hear a lot. Go with it. Let yourself get caught up in the moment a bit. It makes it easier to stay until 3 a.m. if you think it matters. Just leave your high horse at the office when you go home.

LEARN TO TAKE A PUNCH.

I know in this business we talk a lot about being thick-skinned and tough, but it's not only this type of "tough" that is a challenge. You really have to be physically tough and have strong willpower to succeed in this business. Some nights you really put your body through a torture test. Pulling an all-nighter, or finishing up at 3 a.m. and coming in for the 8 a.m. (I call it "the pinch" where the CD responds late at night and the account team plans the meeting early). And even the thick-skinned part of it is more about being calm after the client doesn't like what you spent all that time doing—when you just think, "Man, I could've been sleeping." It's keeping Zen while getting beaten, and smiling, and thanking, and asking for one more shot.

In a contact sport like advertising, you can't flinch, because if you do, that next punch is about to land. Show you're a tough fighter. Sniff up the blood and look them dead in the eye. Fight even harder for a good idea. It'll scare the hell out of them.

On my first real project as an intern, I was asked to write copy for a beer brand. It was still an open brief and they simply wanted to see some long copy to get a sense of where we could take it. From my background I assumed the best place to start would be to do some research about beer. For most this would involve going to the local bar and downing a few, but to me it meant reading about beer. Several hours later I realized I would've been better off going to the bar.

Within the day I had an insightful chunk of copy about the history of beer. Did you know that beer's been around for thousands of years? There are mentions of it going back all the way back to ancient Egypt. Fascinating stuff I assure you.

This was the premise of my first block of copy for the superstar team. A treatise on the birth of the brewing process. I emailed it over to the senior writer on the project for feedback.

An hour later the senior writer came over. He went straight to the other writer intern, Jeff. They began talking specifics on the copy. He was giving the writer all sorts of tips and pointers. He was going through in detail, they were laughing, enjoying themselves. I couldn't wait until it came time for my feedback, I'd waited months for this. My back was ready for patting. The senior writer finished talking to Jeff, it was my turn, but why was he walking away? I blurted out "Did you get a chance to look at my copy?" He did. "Try not to make it sound like a textbook." he said. Then he walked away.

Funny, you signed up
for an agency job
but ended up in politics.

The right way and how to avoid it.

HAVE I BEEN
LIED TO?

Most agencies out there pride themselves on being free of politics. This, of
course, is bullshit. There are politics at every
company, advertising or otherwise.

Navigating the office is necessary for
getting work out the door. Great work can
set you free, but your job will also be about
managing relationships, expectations, and
hallways.

You will be put under unbelievable pressure to meet a deadline. People will threaten hell on Earth if you're even one minute late. Project managers and account teams will call, email, text, and stop by in person. Emails will escalate up to the highest reaches of the account department who will express their sincere and irreversible disappointment in you. Yet, I can't think of a single creative who's ever been fired for asking to push a deadline.

If it's not ready to present, don't you dare present it. Just say, "I understand the deadline is (soon/tomorrow/now), but I can't show work that's not up to the agency's standard. Let's move the meeting."

This might sound irresponsible, but it's quite the opposite. Account teams rarely tell you this, but built into every schedule are multiple rounds of reviews with the client. The lowest number of client reviews I've seen is two, and that was an exceptional case.

Point being, if you take the time to do it right the first time you won't have to redo it a second time. You'll appear responsible and they'll understand why it took longer. If you go into the meeting with unimpressive ideas they will not care that you got it done on time, and at the end of the year when your boss is looking at what you've accomplished, they won't care what the schedule was like.

I'll add a brief warning that your actions will seem poisonous to some. If a person's job is getting work in front of clients on time, there's a fear it will make them appear incapable of doing their jobs.

A second brief warning: let people know as soon as you think you might not make a deadline. Missing a meeting is still unprofessional.

CLIENTS PAY A LOT FOR THE PRIVILEGE OF
KILLING YOUR WORK. LET THEM BE THE
ONES TO DO IT.

If your CD approves it, it's going in front
of the client. Those who disagree can plead
their case with your CDs if they wish, but
that's not your battle. Stand your ground,
lean on the bosses. That's what they're
there for.

People throughout the company have a
vision of what's right. They will be willing
to fight for work they believe in and will
try and make you change work they don't
believe in. They're doing what they in their
hearts think is best for either the brand or
the client relationship (and a lot of times
they're right). But in the end, their opinion
doesn't count. Sorry. You already have a
boss whose job that is.

I've presented work that was "not right"
for the client many times that the client has
then loved.

The more you can coexist with "the other
side," the happier both sides will be, but try
not to let anyone bully you into ruining the
work.

You know the saying, "insanity is doing the same thing over and over and expecting different results?" Advertising is officially insane.

If you ask the same question 20 times, the answer will change. In one of my early weeks I was coming out of a client meeting with crystal-clear feedback. I couldn't argue the points in the meeting, so I went ahead and made the changes. I brought them to my CD who was horrified at all the tweaks I'd made. He pretended the client comments were far smaller than what was said on the call. I thought he was an idiot. Didn't he hear the same call I did?

The final approved ad had just one teensy change that was barely noticeable and the ad was better for it.

In a different meeting, our vendor told us we didn't have time or money to do what we wanted. We talked to the CD about it and he asked for those and even more changes. What a moron!

In the end we had all of those changes and more and the ad was better for it.

Reasonable people don't go very far in advertising. This is an industry for imbeciles.

AS A STARTING CREATIVE, YOUR JOB IS
PROVING YOUR CREATIVE DIRECTOR RIGHT.

You will occasionally get feedback from your CD that you might not agree with. Find a way to make it work. Do the absolute best you can. You can try questioning it if you're deeply opposed, but chances are it's not your gut telling you it's not the right idea, it's your head telling you that you'd rather not do more work since you feel you've already solved it.

Try. See if it works. If you can't crack it, at least you tried and you can go back and explain why it didn't work.

What's crazy about this is that most of the time they will be right. They've been doing it a lot longer than you and have an understanding that you will not have. Also, they are rarely hacks if they've made it to a high post at an award-winning place. You can't climb far if you have fluke success.

There's a lot of arrogance in the business and you can break through just by doing instead of bitching.

There's a reason you got hired at the company. They wanted you. There's something that you do that's necessary for their success. If you're not delivering on it then you're wasting their time, and more importantly, your own. If they fire you for doing what you like to do, oh well, you would never be happy there anyway.

Everyone has some past knowledge or history that they bring to the table. Past jobs or hobbies that define you. Put that into your work and it won't feel like an ad and won't look like anyone else's.

When an ad ends up successful, people get amnesia over which side of it they were on. You'd be amazed how much people who hated your idea suddenly love it. In fact, they clearly remember how hard they worked on it.

If you're crazy about an idea and no-body can convince you otherwise, go for it. Break hearts, go over people's heads, sell it through. If it was a worthwhile idea and it sells, everyone will fall in line rather than look like they were out of touch.

It's false to assume that your job will be any less painful by going with the flow. It's a stressful job no matter what; at least be proud of what you do.

My friend and I have a joke that if you go to the lowest title on award show credits then you see who actually did all of the work. You can tell you're doing great when people start wanting to put their touch on your work. Try your best to keep your idea pure and clean, but be open to letting it get better.

If, however, you worked hundreds of hours, weekends, nights, and then in the last minute somebody wants to put their ink on it and take equal credit, try not to freak out. You can do it again, they can't. They'll be found out and if you work hard enough, so will you.

Feel free to speak up if it makes you feel better, but don't worry, word spreads. It might not be immediate, but within a few years reputations catch up with reality. I've seen it. Huge people can fall if they didn't earn their position.

ACCEPT A GOOD IDEA FROM ANYWHERE.

It shouldn't matter where the idea came from if it's a good idea. If you only allow ideas into the mix that come from your brain, your office, your department, whatever, you're going to be limiting yourself and will come off as kind of a prick. What's worse, in the long run people will lose trust in you as a person with the ability to discern good work from bad work.

PICK SOMEBODY WHO YOU WILL NEVER DISAPPOINT.

All the people I know in the business who've had break-out success have had one person who has become their in-house spokesperson. In exchange, the young professional will kill themselves on every project for that person whether it's a print ad or scanning photos. They never disappoint.

Find that person. Aim as high as you can, but the most important thing is that they love you and you love them.

It will happen to you, as it happens to everybody: you will be spread too thin. No matter how many hours you put in, something will have to give. Make sure it's not on a project from the person championing you.

It's like prison: Become somebody's bitch, or get shanked.

There are only a few thousand people at all the great agencies combined. Within three years you will know at least one person at any place you'd want to work. More importantly, they'll know you. If you're a dick, kiss your career goodbye. In my first year at Goodby Silverstein & Partners, the recruiter asked if I knew so and so from Crispin Porter + Bogusky where I interned. He was a senior art director there when I was just out of school, but his fate was in my hands. Fortunately I liked him and thought he was talented. I said so. I saw him two weeks later around the office.

AVOID DATING
COWORKERS.

You're probably going to ignore this. You might end up getting married to one (which happens a lot). You also might not (which happens a lot more). Either way, compartmentalize the hell out of it. When you cross that door you're a professional in a job, don't let the free beer and casual vibes fool you into thinking it's a single's bar.

Qs and
my As.

Questions I've been asked and
my surly responses.

"Where should I work?"

As I write this part, I'm waiting at the office for my partner. It's 1 a.m., and last night we were here until 2:30 a.m. I'm tired. I'm worn out. I've spent more hours at this place than my home. I don't have some kind of false belief that what I'm doing is critically important to the world. Yet I feel alright. And I'm trying to figure out why. I think a lot of it has to do with the people I work with.

I don't know if I'll work in advertising forever, but I feel fortunate to be around the people I get to be around. They are fun, charming, funny, and stylish.

I can't tell you what it's like to work at a miserable company, because I've never had the patience to stay at one. One fact I can say is that I know people who've come from agencies with frightening reputations and they've been able to leap from there into some of the best agencies in the world. From everything I've heard and seen, I can confidently say the following: talent tends to rise to the top, top-notch people get squeezed out of bad places and just about anywhere you go you will find at least one person who is better than you whom you can learn from.

There is such a heavy focus on the hot shops; the place you work sets the direction for your career in general, but it doesn't matter as much as you think it does. If you're unhappy with a place, don't stay for the name. Nobody else has to be in your job but you.

If you have a job, be happy to be employed; a lot of people aren't. Take it as a sign of how awesome you are. At the same time, if you're not happy, get out. If you want to move somewhere else, make sure you do so out of opportunity, not out of fear or anger.

In that same realm, don't take a job at a place you aren't crazy about for fear that nothing better will come along. I know when I was unemployed for nearly half a year, fresh out of school, it felt like the hardest move to turn down a job. But I wouldn't ever be happy at a place if I settled there because I was afraid.

"I did this shitty thing at a shitty agency, but it was for a big brand. Should I show it?"

I'm sure somebody told you that agencies want to see that you've worked on major clients and produced real work. They don't care. The only thing they are looking for, and ever look for, are people who have ideas and can do the craft.

"I'm a writer, is it ok if the art direction isn't amazing?"

You're a writer and people shouldn't look at art, but I promise you everyone does. I had the same problem with my book coming out of school. The work-around is to get your foot in the door without doing ads, just finding some other way to endear yourself to people. Or some way to make the low visual quality be part of the idea. I heard that a guy once got a job with a book that just had one headline per page, no visual, but 100 pages of killer headlines.

Your book should scare me. I should live in genuine terror of someone finding it and firing my hack ass. You'd be surprised how impressive people's portfolios are even if all they produce in their real careers is crap. Bad ads come from round after round with the client, but in your portfolio, they're perfect.

This industry is competitive to the point where having a stellar portfolio is the requirement of an agency even talking to you. Unless you're related to somebody. If you're not James Omnicom, make that book sing.

What specifically is in a portfolio is always changing, but the basics are the same. You need ideas that are smart. You'll need ads that show you can do your craft. And then you'll need at least one ad that nobody has ever seen before. Do you need digital? Probably. iPhone apps? Sure, why not. But you will want an idea in there that is unheard of and can't be defined.

I remember as an instructor looking at a student's book and telling him that his book was fine and that it was the worst possible situation he could be in. Nothing was wrong with his work and that is precisely what was wrong with it. He couldn't grow because there was nothing to critique and he couldn't get a job because it didn't have that extra level of amazing. I told him to add a campaign that was insane.

Talent is recession proof. If you work honestly and your book is stellar, there will always be a position for you. I know people who were hired at the same time as the company fired huge chunks of the department. Sometimes it takes a little time to find where you ought to be, but that's all it is, a matter of time. In that time, keep your craft sharp.

Ask them.

When I was a student I was sitting on a crowded L train in Chicago. I saw a guy who had an agency's logo on his bag. I asked him if he'd look at my book. He initially said no. A minute later he handed me his business card.

I showed my book to a CD once who told me that there was one and only one ad in my entire book worth keeping.

I went home and put it on my wall, labeled with, "my first ad that doesn't suck."

Ever since then I've made it a habit to mark one ad in my book as my current ad that doesn't suck. Every assignment I do is an attempt to top that piece.

If you look at your book now, I'll bet there is one ad that is clearly the best. Everything else is just decoration for it.

The guy might've been wrong, but the truth is, any book can be better.

How do you get into the business?

Well, I have a whole chapter about this, but no, that's cool. I'll just repeat it.

Getting into the business is half about your work and half about your attitude. And then luck. And then who you know. Actually it's really a 147% game. The trick is to find some way, any way, to stand out from everyone else. It doesn't have to be some huge stunt, you've just got to be a little smarter and a little more persistent than everyone else.

One thought to remember is that a re-cruiter's job is to hire people. If they don't do it and do it well, they're failing at their job. Give them an excuse to bring you in and they will. All they need is something they can point to and say, "This is why I brought this person in to interview."

Turtles.

Super special thanks to:

My wife Jen for marrying me even before I was a published author of an advertising book.

My family in the US and Europe, especially my brother Martin.

My brilliant art director partner and work brother, Josh Engmann, who makes me feel ineloquent and stupid by comparison.

My book designer Anna Kasnyik without whom this beautiful book would be a hideous Word doc.

My mentor Jeff Goodby for writing the foreword and for doing more for my career than I have room to mention here.

Paul Malmstrom, Lauren Ranke, David Kolbusz and Justin Gignac for their kind words.

Special thanks to these people:

Laurence Minsky, my college professor, advisor, and author of a shelf of books.

Veronica Padilla for giving me my first big ad break.

Linda Harless for giving me my next big ad break.

Mary King for giving me my first New York job and moving me across the country.

Susan Holden for reading contracts as if they were in English.

Luke Sullivan, whom I've never met but who wrote the book that got me into advertising. I'll never forgive you.

Thanks to the bosses I've learned the most from (somewhat chronologically):

Alex Bogusky, Andrew Keller, Donnell Johnson, Franklin Tipton, Rob Reilly, Jeff Goodby (again), Rich Silverstein, Steve Simpson, Jamie Barrett, Bob Winter, John Matejczyk (correct spelling), Will McGinness, Mike McKay, Feh Tarty, Pat McKay, Jim Elliott, Mark Wenneker, Jean Sharkey, Tyler Hampton, Marty Senn, Chris Beresford-Hill, Margaret Johnson, Will Elliott, Robert Riccardi, Michael Ian Kaye, Paul Malmstrom (one of the weirdest and most wonderful minds in advertising), Bobby Hershfield, Piers North, Tom Webster, Allon Tatarka, Rob Baird, Charlie McKittrick, Christine Gignac, Scott Hayes, Tim Jones, Bryan Rowles, Tim Wolfe, Rob Teague, Michael Bryce, Matt Curry, Justine Armour, Shanteka Sigers, Kevin Lynch, Stephen Neale.

Thanks to my former art directors for making even my bad ideas look good:

April Lauderdale, Jason Campbell, Antonio Marcato, David Byrd, Andy Babbitz, Jose Luis Martinez, Cris Logan, Sharon Kaye, Karen Land Short, Mandi Lin, Byron DelRosario, Martin Rose, Mike Coyne, Andy Dao, Billy Veasey.

Thanks to a bunch of other people I couldn't have done this without:

David Littlejohn (your move I believe), Ken Miller, EJ Wolborsky, Rob Katzenstein, Nick Zafonte, Jonathan Graham (who overstates my ability to write headlines as well as he does), Mike Aperauch, Ben Rudlin, Mark Rurka, Colleen Hubbard, Erika Ayres, Jillian Fisher, David Girandola, Frannie Rhodes (thanks for letting me hide in your office on rough days), Nathaniel Lawlor (way to wreck the curve for all of us), Scott Norton (my favorite client), Shanita Akintonde, Peg Murphy, Tom Hamilton, Kara Taylor, Dany Lennon, Jerrod New, my accountant Max. All the people I forgot on accident, sorry. All the people I forgot on purpose, quit being paranoid.

Thanks most of all to powerHouse Books for taking a chance on this book and on me.

About the author:

Thomas Kemeny is an award-winning blah blah blah.

He is humbled daily by people who are smarter, funnier, and younger than he is.

www.thomaskemeny.com

About the designer:

Anna Kasnyik is an award-winning blah blah blah.

She is humbled daily by people who are smarter, funnier, and who have twice as many eyebrows as she does.

www.ksnyk.com